WELCOME TO...

THE BITCOIN CAPITAL OF THE WORLD!

THE
BITCOIN CAPITAL

Of The World

BY

JOHN VAN LEYDEN

The Bitcoin Capital is a work of non-fiction. Some characters and persona's, individuals, and events have been changed in order to provide identity protection. Any matter entailed within this book that may resemble someone living or dead unless actual interviewees is purely coincidental and unintentional.

No part of this book may be reproduced in any form without the permission in writing from the author and publisher, except in the case of brief quotations embodied in critical articles or interviews.

Disclaimer: Author and all contributories are not financial advisors and any investment in or related to any matters discussed or promoted in this book will be made at readers or others own risk. Readers of this book except responsibility and liability for their own actions, choices, investments, and lifestyle choices.

Author advises all to seek the advice of their doctor before engaging in any exercise, dieting, or wellness plan and excepts no responsibility of others and their individual actions or choices.

© John Van Leyden

*Cover design: John Van Leyden
*Illustrations/graphics and photography: John Van Leyden
*Editor: Mathew Bennett PhD (Editor and co-founder Cascadia Editors Collective)
*Publisher: John Van Leyden. **All Rights Reserved.**

ISBN-13: 978-1-7336065-0-9 /e-Book
ISBN-13: 978-1-7336065-1-6 /Paperback
ISBN-13: 978-1-7336065-2-3 /Hardcover

DEDICATION

This book is dedicated to my beautiful wife and fun-loving kids. Thank you for supporting me and blessing all my crazy adventures. For enduring and listening to the constant high-tone hum of my Bitcoin mining endeavors. Thank you for letting me take risks, invest in and build computers, mine Bitcoin, and trade cryptocurrencies thus setting the stage for our future... *The Digital Age* to come.

Thank you to the United States of America for giving me the freedom to be a Bitcoin miner and the freedom of speech to write and publish this book.

Thank you God, for my life...and please bless those in need with prosperity and riches.

TABLE OF CONTENTS

Teaser
Introduction

Chapter 1 : The Road to Success
Chapter 2 : So what the heck is Bitcoin and Where did it come from?
Chapter 3 : The Critical Components of Bitcoin Mining
Chapter 4 : How to Build a Bitcoin Mining Operation
Chapter 5 : How to Start Mining Bitcoins
Chapter 6 : Bitcoin Mining as a Career
Chapter 7 : The Bitcoin Capital of the World
Chapter 8 : Keep Your Finger on the Pulse
Chapter 9 : Upgrading a Bitcoin Mining Operation
Chapter 10: Grayscale
Chapter 11: Cryptocurrencies
Chapter 12: Blockchain
Chapter 13: Bitcoin in Use
Chapter 14: The Digital Age
Chapter 15: How to Achieve Health, Wealth, and Wellness.
Chapter 16: Retire and Mine Bitcoin
Chapter 17: A Visionary's Perspective

Conclusion
Bible Verses
References and Recommendations
Index

BITCOIN CAPITAL

Bitcoin: Bit•coin | \'bit-,koin | a digital currency created for use in peer-to-peer online transactions.

Capital: cap•i•tal | \'ka-p-tel | 1) being the seat of government, or chief in importance or influence; 2) a store of useful assets or advantages.
(Merriam-Webster Dictionary, 11th ed.)

Capital: Also know as wealth in the form of money or other assets used to generate income. Capital makes the business world go 'round because it reflects and determines what is bought and sold in an economy.
(www.Merriam-Webster.com/dictionary/capital)

TEASER

"SOMETHING IS HAPPENING... SOMETHING WORLD CHANGING. CAN YOU SEE IT?"

The world's first trillionaire will be born from Bitcoin. There is no more powerful, volatile, and leverageable asset on earth like it. Bitcoin has the potential to dwarf the likes of Microsoft, Apple, IBM, Google, Amazon, and other current technological assets. There is no comparable investment vehicle on earth the has the potential for astronomical future growth.

Gold is tapped out!
Oil is old news!

The Internet is the now, the future, and Bitcoin is the fuel to run it.

Teaser

To paraphrase a famous quotation:

One coin to rule them all
One coin to find them
One coin to bring them all
And in the darkness bind them.

Not even the discovery for the cure for cancer could create the world's first trillionaire. A development of a reproducible fusion or hydrogen vehicle? Maybe hundreds of billions. Discovery of an untapped store of gold will only increase its supply and thus bring down the value. The same can be said for oil or any other natural resource, commodity, or product. If the supply is increased the value will decrease.

This is **Economics 101**: *The law of supply and demand.*

That is not the case for Bitcoin. There can never be more than 21 million Bitcoins.

21 Million... That is it! No more.

You cannot tap a new well or mine any Bitcoins beyond 21 million. The supply of Bitcoin cannot be increased therefore the value can only rise exponentially over time. If Bitcoin becomes the world's accepted store of value, then the potential is as follows...

Currently the net worth of the world is 250 trillion. I personally believe it's much higher, perhaps in the quadrillions if you include every asset, fund, property, business, government, etc. on (or rotating around) the earth.

Let's stick with 250 trillion for now.

When all things of value on earth are traded with one universal store of value, that would be Bitcoin for this hypothetical example. The value of one Bitcoin would be near 12 million US dollars. That said, one might predict the future value of Bitcoin, based on current world wide net worth, to rise to at least $12,000,000 USD each.

$12,000,000 a Bitcoin!

Bitcoin is an international worldwide phenomenon. No one person, country, or government controls it. It is owned by the people, controlled peer to peer, and with no middleman or bank to steal or skim from your value or wealth.

The smart nations or governments of the world will sooner or later realize this and get on the band wagon. Those who accept customers of Bitcoin, Bitcoin miners, and Bitcoin investments will be able to monetize them fair and square. First come, first served.

Those entities that try to ban, criminalize, place a moratorium on, or shut down Bitcoin mining, trading, smart contracts, blockchains, or cryptocurrency development are taking away our Constitutional/(USA) and universal right to freedom, prosperity, and commerce. They will be met with worldwide resistance, lawsuits, and ultimately failure. No one entity can stop or control what the people of the world choose to use for a store of value, plug in to their power outlets, trade and barter for, or use their Internet service for. If you are paying your power and Internet bills and are safely within the constraints of your homes infrastructure, then what you choose to power or stream legally is your business. This is called privacy.

People are sick and tired of watching their hard-earned money go down in value each time their government decides to print more money. Governments are only able to do this due to the fiat currency system that is currently in place. Fiat money has no intrinsic value, is decreed to be legal tender by the government, and has an infinite supply. This is not the case with Bitcoin. There are only 21 million Bitcoins and will only be 21 million. The supply of Bitcoin is fixed. Bitcoin gives each and every one of us protection against this watering down of our wealth. Bitcoin is the hedge against deflation, stagnation, and inflation of money. Bitcoin cannot be duplicated, or the quantity increased. When Bitcoin becomes the world's store of value for all nations, you can bet that when a consumer good goes up in price it is real value behind it that is driving up the price.

Again, the smart nations of the world will make every effort to embrace Bitcoin, blockchain, and cryptocurrency technological breakthroughs with open arms and figure out how to capitalize on it.

The world's first zillionaire will be a nation and it will be due to their early adoption, investment in, infrastructure development, application of, monetization, and capitalization of Bitcoin and the Bitcoin blockchain.

Teaser

Did you know that the number one selling book in history is the Bible and it references money over 800 times? Another amazing fact is that Jesus offers more wisdom in matters on money than any other subject in his teachings second to the "Kingdom of God."

(Pastor Mike Wilson: 1:06:19 live.sagehillschurch.com)

Money is one of the most significant forces in our lives and an important thing to take seriously. In the history of humanity there have been uncountable different forms of money, currencies, coins, and stores of value. Bitcoin is next on the list. The next stage in the evolution of money.

A photo of Fox Business currencies banner...USD compared to Bitcoin before any other world currency.

Spondoolies SP31 Bitcoin Miners

INTRODUCTION

"FROM GARBAGE MAN TO BITCOIN TYCOON"

Every person on this earth has a chance to grab a piece of the pie. Everybody can work, invest, take risks, and work some more. In these early years of Bitcoin development there will be many ups and downs, hiccups, and turmoil. This will cause the value of Bitcoin to fluctuate in a volatile nature for years to come. The time to get in is now, tomorrow, and at every future opportunity. Hopefully you get in during the Bitcoin lows, not too late in the game when the value becomes astronomical—so astronomical that the chance to turn a hundred dollars into a hundred thousand dollars will be long past.

Bitcoin (BTC) could become worthless. Just like any store of value it can be denied by the world. But as of now, as Yoda would say, "embracing Bitcoin, the world is." Watch any major news channel and USD/BTC is the leading currency ticker of

Introduction

all currency banners. Just turn on the boob tube and see it with your own eyes on Fox Business, CNNMoney, CNBC, and others. All run financial reports with currency banners listing Bitcoin slashed with the US dollar. This is a statement, my friends. Bitcoin First! Always First! I believe this is a telling of things to come, and the inextricable link or relationship between BTC and USD.

Life is passing by at lightning speed and the end is coming much too soon for all of us. During my years so far as an occupation therapist(OT), I have interviewed thousands of patients, and there exists a common theme among the elders I meet: *being poor sucks and, often, having poor physical health contributed to their current predicament.*

In this book I want to tell you my story from a PC gamer and welfare boy to garbage man to bodybuilder, then personal trainer, OT, real estate investor and Bitcoin miner living in The Bitcoin Capital of the World (Douglas County, WA). I'm on the road to health & wellness...and wealth? You betcha. Just how much wealth we'll know in the future digital age to come.

I am laying the foundation for my future. I'm making investments in my body, my education and knowledge base, but also in real estate, business, 401(k), IRA, social media, and Bitcoin assets. The investments I am making are laying the foundation for my health, wellness, and wealth as well as a well-funded retirement ahead.

I've made a few mistakes so far and I've also had a few successes in this wonderful journey called life. I want to share some of the blunders that I witnessed my good friend Pedro make in his journey to become a Bitcoin miner, and some of the colorful characters who helped me on my path to becoming a Bitcoin miner myself. I want you to be successful on your journey working toward a happy, wealthy, and healthy future.

In this book, I'm going to talk about my roots, my life experiences, and how the heck I started mining Bitcoin. I currently maintain a healthy body through diet and exercise, and at the same time work full time, plus extra time writing this book and making investments. That's not to mention mining Bitcoin and taking care of all family responsibilities! I want to share my knowledge and expertise on the human body and motivate you to take action toward your personal health and wellness. I've also had success planning and building a successful home-based Bitcoin mining operation, and I want to share some of my experience and knowledge so you can start your own Bitcoin mining farm. I have learned that you have to build the base of cash flowing assets from the bottom up when you start out dead broke with no family bailouts. It's a bit slow going but totally worth the effort. For one, I believe the old saying…

"Money can't bring you happiness"

…is total BS.

This is said by people who have money already. It's used to brainwash poor children to distract their thoughts and feelings from their deprivation. To be perfectly frank, being poor is exactly that—poor! By definition, being poor is…

Lacking sufficient money to live at a standard considered comfortable or normal in a society.

This poverty dilemma for me built strength of character and the drive to want more, to work harder for more, and to take the necessary steps to achieve change. When I was about 10 years old, after school and on the weekends, I would walk through alleyways and streets for miles collecting aluminum cans and then walk the bags of cans to the recycling center and trade them in for cash.

Introduction

My philosophical point: growing up in poverty as a welfare kid anticipating your single mom's monthly welfare check to go shopping while wearing other kid's discarded clothes...It absolutely sucks and wears you thin! Living on happy thoughts, dumpster diving for aluminum cans, positive reinforcement from my mother, family and faith are the glue that held me together in those tough years. Plus, the fact that we live in a free country and I grew up believing that I had a chance to make things better for myself if I chose to do the work, work hard, and take risks. I believe that making money and being healthy are symbiotic in nature. You can't have one without the other and maintain a good quality of life.

Douglas County, home now and the **Bitcoin Capital of the World** was a different environment twenty years ago. Mostly agriculture landscape, wheat fields as far as the eye can see, in the recent years is experiencing the quiet and low key but rapid building of Internet infrastructure, power, business, and housing. In fact, north central Washington State is a different beast entirely compared to the years of my welfare youth.

The neighboring county, Chelan, sits directly across the wide, cold, Columbia River from Douglas County has long been considered the Apple Capital of the World. Now apple orchards are being bull dozed and replaced with housing.

On up the Columbia River, north of Chelan and Douglas counties is Okanogan County, then the Canadian border. This central corridor (referred to as North Central Washington) is seeing a massive overhaul in infrastructure, housing, and commerce. The change in central Washington is due an influx of California and western Washington residents selling their homes and relocating to a beautiful, mild weathered, and rewarding area, north central Washington.

You can't blame them though. They can sell their high priced homes and then buy acreage, build their dream home

Introduction

with breathtaking views of the mountains, rivers, and all for a fraction of the money from the sale of their old home. Then have a motherload of money in the bank to afford retirement.

Douglas County has seen a massive infrastructure build out of wind turbine farms, hydroelectric power, and substations to power data centers, databases, and Bitcoin mining farms.

Douglas County is a Bitcoin miner's heaven due to the overabundance of power and (to date) Bitcoin and tech friendly atmosphere. This is why I and others deem Douglas County The Bitcoin Capital of the World. I'll be filling you in with more details about north central Washington and Douglas County later on in this book.

Back in the day, I had a few things that entertained me and kept me and my brothers and sisters out of trouble.

—First was the outdoors. We played, made forts, cycled, and explored the environment around whatever subsidized rental we were living in at the time.

—Second was television. Can you say cartoons, movies, family chill time? Cartoons are just pure fun and entertaining for kids, movies and sitcoms let you see other people's lives and situations, then you can envision a better life for yourself as you grow up building the internal drive to succeed and live better.

—The third was and is (in a limited capacity in my aging years): video games. Ah, video games. Video games take you to a different place. An imaginative world with unlimited potential. They keep you engaged, thinking, problem solving, and having fun.

It all started with the Super Nintendo Entertainment System, then on to PlayStation and Xbox. After high school I graduated to personal computer gaming, or PC gaming. I fell in love with the immersive digital graphics and intense gameplay of PC gaming. I taught myself how computers were built and started building and programming my own gaming computers.

My kids call my younger brother Uncle Dirt now. Well, when we were younger, I watched him fall in love with video gaming too. He lived a bit less actively then me, however. In fact, he lived the opposite. I played video games, worked, and remained physically active. He, on the other hand, was very sedentary and blew up in size like the Goodyear Blimp over the course of high school. Uncle Dirt was a cool laid-back dude, dressed for comfort, and with a simple life philosophy: video games, movies, and take-out food means life is good. Uncle Dirt would get off school and then work an hour at our small town video store to earn a free video game. Then on the way home he would stop by Safeway and grab a two-for-one pizza deal. He'd take that home eat it and play video games all from the comfort of his recliner without a movement (other than to race to the bathroom at the precipice of a potential urine geyser or pissing of the pants).

I love my brother and it was a bit concerning to see a healthy boy turn into an obese young adult so quickly. But I learned by my brother's example what not to do in order to stay healthy. There's a silver lining to this story. I helped my brother get in the best shape of his life later on in his young adulthood, and it is that plan for transformation that I want to share with you.

I was always intrigued with physiques like Arnold Schwarzenegger's and Sylvester Stallone's. I had early interest in weight training and trying to achieve those iconic physical attributes. I read the Encyclopedia of Modern Bodybuilding by Arnold Schwarzenegger. This book opened up an idea that bodybuilding would help me achieve my goals in life. And it did! Arnold is absolutely right about bodybuilding helping a person learn discipline, about ways to earn the physical reward

Introduction

of muscles and strength, and how to set goals and achieve them. These attributes of bodybuilding transferred over into all other aspects of life for me. It set me on a path to learn, earn, and successfully achieve my goals and dreams. Arnold talks about happiness being linked to physical health and wellness as well as working hard, setting life goals, and striving to achieve them.

Like writing this book: I had a dream, I set a long-term goal and many short-term goals, I made a plan to achieve all those goals, and then I did the work. Voila! The book is written, edited, published, and now it is in your hands. I have learned over the years that one should strive to achieve a balance of fun, work, and health by staying active, making investments, building up an arsenal of assets, and taking risks.

•

What the hell do we have to lose?

•

Life is short and before you know it is over.

•

Do you want to go through life a toadstool in the dark, a bump on a log, or a corpse zombie wandering through life aimlessly? Or do you want to grow into the light of the sun, to rise up out of the ashes of an aimless vision?

—Do you want to be somebody that bears the burden of regret?

—Regret of not taking risks? Regret of not following your dreams?

—Regret of not taking care of your body and having poor health?

—Regret of not preparing for your future?

Introduction

We should strive to have the least amount of regret in our lives.

This is a belief shared by Jeff Bezos creator of Amazon, which I'll go into more later.

Looking back on the development of my life from uninformed, naive, and eager welfare kid to the present, I see what I lacked was an ability to see the future and the possibilities. Until I educated myself and had life experiences, I was stuck in an uneducated, unskilled, and unprovoked state of knowledge and asset poverty. Until I learned from others, grew through experience, and sought out the necessary knowledge for myself, I was unable to achieve my dreams. I was stuck in that place of poverty that I was born and raised in. Not a good starting point but a starting point nonetheless.

Knowledge is key. Developing skill sets is a tool for success. Education is the fundamental asset for all things to come. Education develops skill sets, skill sets are valuable to the world, and you will get paid for your value.

I would likely never have and would not be a Bitcoin miner now had it not been for my knowledge of computers and how to build them, which stemmed from my years PC gaming.

I first started mining Bitcoin in 2009. Being a PC gamer and computer geek the idea that you could use your computer to run a program to search or "mine" the Internet for money was intriguing. Intriguing was the fact that these Bitcoins had a value and yet they were essentially free. Keep in mind that this also a time in history of the devastating financial crisis, the Deep Recession when the house bubble burst, the price of gas doubled, and banks went bankrupt. Trust in the banks and currencies of the world were at an all-time low. So, when I first heard about Bitcoin, Bitcoin mining, and the potential value of Bitcoin…Well, I was all in.

At the time it was known that there were 21 million

Introduction

Bitcoins out there in cyberspace and the cost to have them was computing power and electricity. It was a first-come, first-served basis and I wanted to be at the head of the line.

The computer I first used to mine Bitcoin was a custom gaming computer that I built myself. I've been a PC gamer since the late 1990s when Unreal Tournament, then after Halo had overtaken the typical console game graphics and controls. This is also at a time when the Internet was booming into mainstream existence and used by most people. The ability to learn how to do anything was at our fingertips, a few mouse clicks and a search engine away. (If you haven't built your own computer, I highly recommend it. It is much easier than imagined and is a rewarding learning experience.)

I named my computer at the time The Viper because the case I used for the build was an XG red Viper case, one of the coolest computer cases I've ever seen. It was a large ATX aluminum case with the word Viper across the side wall, similar in font to the Dodge Viper. The front of the case had a large snake head looking right at you. When turned on, it had a digital viper head, LED lighting, and a fan control display. What a head turner!

I did my research and downloaded the Bitcoin mining program, the Bitcoin QT. The program seemed a bit archaic, spitting out lines of numbers and computer language. Being a little paranoid about computer hacking, spyware, phishing schemes, and Internet viruses, I did not like the concept of leaving my beautiful Viper gaming computer running 24 hours a day, 7 days a week on the Internet. But I did it anyways.

I started the Bitcoin mining program and left for work. I checked on the computer and mining operation every day after work. I was amassing hundreds of Bitcoins out of thin air basically, but there was nothing I could do with them (or conceive to do with them) that amounted to any real value. At the end of the work week on a Friday afternoon I was chomping at the bit to do some PC gaming. I didn't want the Bitcoin mining process to put any lag on my gaming, so I shut down the program and gamed away.

This was a life choice I made that has left me with regret ever since.

I never turned the Bitcoin mining program back on. In fact, I don't know how many total Bitcoins I mined. After 5 days of mining 24 hours a day, I figure I had earned hundreds maybe thousands of Bitcoins. I don't know now and I didn't care then. At the time I was more worried about getting a virus on my computer, burning out the motherboard or the processor due to the mining causing the Viper to run pretty darn hot. It was fun, but at the time there was no financial benefit worth the risk of burning up my computer or getting a computer virus. I loaded Halo, became Master Chief, and shot me some aliens.

At the time I did not have a full understanding of what Bitcoin really was and the potential of something like blockchain. I did not have a vision of the future of Bitcoin and blockchain technology, or even an inkling of an idea of how it would eventually captivate the world in years to come.

Later in 2010, I made a killer deal trading my Viper gaming computer, two Honda Odyssey dune buggies, a pocket bike, and some cash for a cool and rare 1984 Grumman semi-truck and trailer rig. It was an old Frito Lay delivery setup. I had found the Grumman tractor-trailer setup on a Craigslist ad and made the deal with a retired US Marshal from Mukilteo, WA. He was a bit secretive and not forthcoming about much, other than that he really just needed to get the Grumman off his property. He said he planned to keep the dune buggies for his grandkids and give the Viper to his daughter for college.

Boy what I wouldn't do to get that Viper rig back! I'm always regretting that I did not continue Bitcoin mining and wish I still had that Viper computer. I could be retired, playing online PC games on a 6 screen computer system, or catching some

Introduction

sunshine on a beach in Hawaii. I wonder how many Bitcoins I had in the Bitcoin wallet stored on the hard drive of that Viper gaming computer? They definitely have "value" now and are worth thousands if not millions of dollars.

The Viper had Windows Vista, an obsolete operating system nowadays. If the Viper is still in existence (and not in a landfill), it has most likely been wiped clean and reformatted by now. But before it could be wiped, back when Bitcoin surged in value, I made an effort to retrieve it.

I attempted to find those old contact numbers, looking for old notes or any data on that US Marshal to see if he would be willing to sell me back the Viper computer for sentimental reasons. I was willing to pay a premium, of course, but I could not find the contacts, or remember his name and address. I thought about hiring a private investigator, as it would be worth the investment if it was retrieved, but the chances of finding it without the knowledge of who the US Marshal was seemed like a no-win situation to me. At the time, I could not afford to investigate and lose.

I posted a want ad on Craigslist in the multiple areas of Washington state with a picture of the red Viper gaming computer, but the only leads were frauds, scammers, and catfishers (bottom dwelling low life scum suckers of the Internet).

So, if you happen to stumble upon a red Viper computer case, the contents inside might still hold Bitcoins in a wallet. dat file on the hard drive. It could be a major score. And if you're a retired US Marshal reading this book, I'll trade back that Grumman semi, no questions asked!

I wasn't interested in Bitcoin again until the winter of 2014. Bitcoin was just coming off a boom and crash and making news around the world. Bitcoin appreciated exponentially in 2013. News of the Silk Road and Dread Pirate Roberts debacle, the rapid growth spurt of Bitcoin in 2013, and the understanding of the scarcity of 21 million coins put Bitcoin back on the radar.

Over the next five years I was not idle. I gained experience in real estate, business, retirement investments, health and wealth building in that time. I had a better understanding of the development of technology and technology markets, including Bitcoin, which was leading to the digital age. I could see the laws of economics unfolding right in front of my eyes with the economy, the price of gas, housing, automobiles, etc.

The law of supply and demand is real, and I realized the potential of Bitcoin due to its scarcity.

I am an avid investor in high risk penny stocks and dabble in higher risk 401(k) investment funds. This is how I roll! I love investing in things on the ground floor and seeing what happens. I buy lottery tickets, enter prize drawings, and buy raffle tickets at every opportunity

...and of course I am also invested in the lower risk...lower volatility assets, but there are plenty of books on them and they're well known already. Bitcoin is new and exciting!

CHAPTER ONE

THE ROAD TO SUCCESS

Before we get into how I started my Bitcoin mining operation I want to set the stage on the importance of doing the research, studying, and educating one's self before investing. Knowledge is at your fingertips nowadays.

Most successful entrepreneurs or tech developers built their products off much knowledge and experience. I believe it is important to take care of your mind and body in on this path to a rewarding future. By far the most valuable asset I have and continue to invest in is my education. And you should too.

The more I educate myself, the more skilled and knowledgeable I am, thus the more leverage I have to help me succeed in achieving my goals and dreams. My advice? Read everything in sight! Now, I'm not talking about novels; I haven't read one of those since they made me in high school. I'm talking about books that teach you something about health and wealth.

I'm talking about books written by the most successful and smart people in the world, the innovators, inventors, leaders, movers and shakers. If you want to become rich read books by rich people like Robert Kiyosaki, Warren Buffett, Donald Trump, Daymond John, Gary Vaynerchuk, Dave Ramsey, Tony Robbins, and Suze Orman. If you want to achieve a great physique read books by people that are lean, healthy, and obviously walk the talk. I recommend books by Arnold Schwarzenegger, The Zone Diet by Barry Sears, The Essential Atkins for Life Kit by Robert Atkins, Transcend by Ray Kurzweil and Terry Grossman. These books will give you good ideas.

It is your job to put these ideas into practice and incorporate them into your lifestyle. It is 100% on you whether or not you read books, eat lean, and exercise to achieve a healthy body. The more educated a person is, the higher salary they command. Education equals mental skills. Mental skills equals skilled labor. The more skilled you are, the more valuable an asset you become to yourself and others.

Nowadays, we are getting constant mixed messages on education. Can you imagine growing up in today's age where we glorify the high school or college drop out? Some of the most successful and famous people in America did not complete their high school or college education. These people and their circumstances are rare. I guarantee that people that drop out of school and become successful have learned knowledge and ideas in an area of focus they are passionate about. I would also bet that these rare few do the work and, in fact, work their

Chapter One

asses off to achieve their success in their field.

Take Bill Gates, the owner/creator of Microsoft. He's well known for dropping out of college and becoming one of the most successful and wealthiest people in the world. Well, this is a mixed message because he did learn a foundation of education. He did complete high school (12 years of education) and, not only that, he rocked high school and achieved a score of 1590 out of 1600 on the SATs. He completed two years of college at one of the most prestigious universities in America, Harvard. This is a total of 14 years of education. Who knows what other knowledge he gained by reading books, working on computers as a kid, or playing around with coding and software development?

Steve Jobs, the co-founder of Apple, is another example of misleading drop out success. He too finished 12 years of education with a high school diploma, one year or partial year in college, plus a year or two studying Zen Buddhism. He had completed about 15 years of education before taking the plunge on an idea about computers.

Mark Zuckerberg, the creator/owner of Facebook, is one of the richest people on earth and well known for "dropping out of school." This is again another misleading and false narrative for our youth. He too amassed a breadth of education and knowledge, including 12 years earning a high school diploma. Not only that, during high school he excelled in classes and was transferred to a private school where he won prizes in mathematics, astronomy, and physics. He also attended the prestigious John Hopkins Center for Talented Youth summer camp. By the time he applied to college he could read and write in French, Hebrew, Latin, and ancient Greek. While Zuckerberg was young, his father taught him Atari basic programming. His father also hired a tutor in software development to work with Mark privately. Mark took graduate-level college classes on software development while still in high school. He worked

Chapter One

on other projects in software engineering, as well as creating his own company, Intelligent Media Group. All while still in high school. He went on to complete one year and then a partial second year of college at Harvard. The idea that Mark Zuckerberg "dropped out" of college and became successful is highly misleading. He had amassed a crazy amount of experiences, educating himself and working his ass off in his areas of focus, his passion: software development. These are just a few examples of successful rich people who "dropped out of school." No wonder so many people nowadays are so confused, lost, unemployed, and failing. They have been misled to believe that you can get something out of nothing. They have been misled to believe that school and education are not necessary to achieve success, that "dropping out" is a viable path to becoming one of the richest persons in history. Education was in fact the backbone to these billionaires success.

My story? I had a rough start financially. I was raised by a single mother on welfare until I left home after graduating from high school. I had to work to earn money during most of my youth for anything I wanted beyond food, water, and second-hand clothing. Working after school and summers hindered my ability to learn. I had to take summer school to meet my graduation requirements. I barely passed and only by the hair of my chinny-chin-chin earned my high school diploma. I went on to the community college and ended up dropping out because I had failed English 81 twice! English 81 was the required class before you were allowed to take your first basic college level class, English 101. I also could not afford to not work. Financially, I was screwed. I had no outside or parental financial assistance and could not afford rent, car insurance, and all the expenses of life, let alone college.

My cheap car breaking down was the final dagger.

I ended up dropping out of college to work 6 a.m. to noon as the dough master for Pizza Hut and then as a garbage truck

Chapter One

washer from 2 p.m. to 10:30 p.m. Monday through Friday. I worked a third job on Saturday and Sunday at Kentucky Fried Chicken. I also was back living with my mom, brothers and sisters. I was the oldest of five kids. All stuck in the welfare lifestyle. I had never been taught the skills to do anything special or unique, other than flip burgers or scoop ice cream.

I landed an opportunity as the truck washer at Waste Management and started to learn how to drive septic trucks to earn my commercial driver's license (CDL). I worked my way up the ladder. I earned my CDL and new skills driving a septic truck and sucking out portable toilets and septic tanks with my big suck-wand and 50-foot hose. I loved this job. Waste Management had become the parental void I needed to earn a great income, stay out of trouble, and learn about health insurance, 401(k)s, safety issues, customer service, taxes, personal responsibility, and productivity. I soon leveled up from lowly shit sucker to full garbage man, and for the first time in my life I was financially secure and happy. (*Thank you, Waste Management, for all the training and re-training, for investing in an unskilled but eager and motivated 19-year-old welfare boy. I am so grateful*).

I worked for Waste Management from 19 to 27 years old. I amassed a great deal of knowledge and skills working for this company. I saved $34,000 in my 401(k), owned my own truck, but was thirsty for more. I've always wanted more! When you're raised on welfare, all you want is more. By this time, I realized that I wasted my time in high school. Rather than putting in the necessary work to learn professional skills, I was focused on having more girlfriends and parties. In high school, I worked as many hours after school and on weekends as I could in order to afford an unaffordable partying lifestyle. I had a cheap car and a lot of fun, but not enough education to do more after high school. That's why I did not succeed in my

Chapter One

first attempt at college.

At 26 years old I had learned many lessons on life and personal responsibility. While I worked full time at Waste Management, I began attending college after work. This time I aced that English 81 class because I was finally doing the homework and really studying my ass off. I also aced that Math 95 class and finally advanced to my first entry-level college classes, English and Math 101. I had learned the basics to give a college degree another try if I wanted to. From that point on I became a college class steam roller. At one point I had to get approval from the dean of the college to take 34 college credits simultaneously. I did this by taking 21 credits at the college and 13 more through correspondence and online classes. An overload for sure but I was dedicated.

By age 27 I earned my associate's degree in science, or AAS, all while attending night school and working full time as a garbage man. I had a passion to earn a bachelor's degree and move on to a better career and higher income. I was still a welfare boy at heart and remained in a situation where everything relied on me. No one person to bail me out if I needed financial assistance. Quitting my job at Waste Management was necessary if I was to be successful at a four-year university. What a scary decision to make. To leave a great job with income, medical, and retirement benefits was the most difficult decision to make.

By the time I was accepted to a four year college, I was prepared to quit my job at Waste Management and I did just that. I was able to make this decision because of three simple reasons:
—I had deep passion to learn and earn more.
—I had no debt and owned my car.
—I had saved $34,000 in my 401(k) retirement plan.

Chapter One

The most important of these three was and is passion. Passion is the fuel that leads to dreams coming true. The second most important is freedom from debt. Debt is a make-or-break situation. A person in debt is a person who cannot break free until the debt is paid off. Do you own your own car or do you own a loan? With debt, do you really own yourself?

The third reason for my ability to take the plunge, quit my job, and go for a university degree is that I had money in the bank. While at Waste Management I had saved $34,000 in my 401(k). At that time it was 1999, so this was a good chunk of change to invest in myself and a college degree.

I want to say with great appreciation, "Thank you to the US government for allowing me to use my 401(k) money for college and necessary living expenses without early withdrawal penalty." I was able to accomplish this by rolling my 401 (k) into an IRA, which does not incur the 10% early withdrawal fee and at the level I was withdrawing as I needed it for college I remained below the income tax threshold. Basically I was at poverty level income during college. I am very grateful that I was able to use my retirement money and put it toward earning my college degree.

With my college degree I learned a great deal of skills in an area of focus and landed a high-paying career in a hospital as an occupational therapist with great medical benefits, vacation pay, and more continuing education opportunities.

The stage was now set, I had saved up some seed money and decided to invest in real estate. I read everything on real estate I could get my hands on. To date I've bought and sold many properties for a great profit. I have rentals and continue to let them pay for themselves. I remodeled two with my own bare hands. How did I learn the skills? I read many books on the subject of construction, remodeling, and probably watched a few thousand YouTube videos titled "how to."

What I have learned and continue to practice is that it

Chapter One

doesn't matter who you are or where you come from, if you have a passion to do something, all you have to do is read books on the subject, watch instructional videos, and search the Internet to gain the knowledge necessary to do that something! ANYTHING!!! Nowadays, free-flowing information is right there at the tap your fingertip or the point of your remote.

When it came to my first plunge at investing in real estate it was a HUGE learning curve. I had zero knowledge about it, but I did the work of learning the skills and conquered it. A few of the most rewarding and educational experiences I have had was...

Selling a condo "For Sale by Owner (FSBO)." I learned how to deal in sale price, how to draw up the real estate paperwork and/or contracts, and how to do business with a title company. What I learned from this experience is that hiring a Realtor is not necessary but an expensive luxury and without the use of a Realtor you get to keep all that commission money for yourself, which for a $250,000 sale is about an extra $15,000 in your pocket.

Applying for a commercial real estate loan. Commercial anything is a whole different beast than residential in realms of real estate and business. I learned how to write up a business plan for real estate, deal with commercial bankers, and commercial real estate appraisers. A nice trick I learned was to not use your own Realtor but the sellers agent and in the purchase and sales agreement negotiate in for 3% back at closing. We actually got paid $4,500 to buy the building. I'm telling you, you don't need a Realtor...the service is an expensive luxury. Don't get me wrong I've have paid for a Realtors services in the past because of how complicated and unusual a couple deals were...but I paid a premium for their help. Sometimes a Realtor is worth it—most of the time not.

Remodeling a commercial building. I purchased a 3200 square foot 2 story retail store in the downtown corridor.

Chapter One

This was my first real estate investment. My wife and I both worked, saved some money, and borrowed seed money from our parents, which we paid back over the next 5 years. I did most of the demolition and build up, framing to finish by myself and with the help of much family team work. I learned how to deal with and manage sub contractors and laborers on a few of the specialty jobs like sheet rock, plumbing, and electrical. When the building was completed we put it for lease and have been collecting continuous rent for over 13 years thus far. This is called sweat equity as over time the property is appreciating in value and someone else is paying our mortgage.

Because of the learning and experiences I've had in real estate investments, I have no more fear and look forward to the next real estate opportunity. Even if the opportunity is different from the one I've experienced, I know I can read, watch, listen, and learn what is necessary to help me succeed in my goals and dreams.

On the road to health, wealth, and wellness (health & wealthness: my mantra or aim for a happy life), I would have to say that work— that is, the blood, sweat, and tears you put into something—is the #1 most important attribute you must express.

When someone asks you (and trust me, they will!), "How can Bitcoin have value for nothing?" The answer is simple. There is a ton of work and energy that has been expended to create or mine each individual Bitcoin. First, there is the research and development (R&D) that went into the creation of Bitcoin, the Bitcoin algorithms, protocols, and blockchain technology. A brilliant and shadowy person (or entity) by the name of Satoshi Nakamoto is behind the vision, design, and implementation of Bitcoin and blockchain existence. Of note, most of the world believes Satoshi to be one person, but Satoshi could be a group of people, a government body, a nation, or even an extraterrestrial.

Chapter One

Aside from the initial work—the R&D, plus the implementation by Satoshi Nakamoto—there is the work of Bitcoin mining that is necessary to bring each Bitcoin out of its encryption womb and into the world to play...just like a newborn baby.

CHAPTER TWO

SO WHAT THE HECK IS BITCOIN AND WHERE DID IT COME FROM?

Trade of goods and services is and always will be an action to obtain the necessities and excessities of life. For most it is necessary for survival. Money has existed for over 2700 years that we know of and can be divided into two main attributes, "money of account" (a ledger of credits and debits) and "money of exchange" (hard medium of exchange made from metal, wood, or other composite). Bitcoin is both a ledger of credits and debits...the blockchain, and a medium of

Chapter Two

exchange in the form of a digital currency...Bitcoin.

The invention of money was never recorded or written about in human history so how it was originally developed is of a logical perspective or theoretical reference. Money in itself has no value unless that money is actually made out of something of value, like a gold or silver coin. Money that has no intrinsic value is considered a fiat currency. Fiat currency is any form of money that has been established as money by the players in the economy. Fiat money can represent a value of/or be backed by something of tangible value like gold, silver, or any other commodity.

A fiat currency can also be backed by a non-tangible or no value source like a government, people, or parties engaging in exchange agree on its value. The US dollar is a fiat currency because it itself is only worth the paper it's printed on and has value determined by the governments and nations of the world. A fiat currency is controlled by the government that backs it. That government can create or print more money at any time they deem necessary. When a government prints more money, as the quantity of money increases, coincidently the value of that money decreases and the price of goods and services will rise to compensate. This is called inflation. If a government prints money too fast or recklessly, that money can eventually become worthless if the people of the nation lose faith in its value.

Bitcoin is a fiat currency and the first currency of its kind to be adopted by the world that comes with its own accounting ledger and a token of non-intrinsic value. Bitcoin is also fixed at 21,000,000 and can never be increased by any entity. If someday a hacker or other entity is able to increase the supply of Bitcoin, then it would be on the same grounds as the majority of the worlds currencies as they exist today. This is not the case though. At this time Bitcoin has demonstrated high security from counterfeiting or duplication, thus at a fixed 21,000,000

Chapter Two

Bitcoins is extremely scarce in the world of money.

In the traditional monetary system people use accountants, banks, online, and paper accounting systems. All of these systems can be corrupted, edited, or manipulated by the people that control them. This cannot happen with the Bitcoin blockchain accounting ledger. The blockchain records any and all transactions between paying and receiving parties and then stores the transactions on millions of computers around the globe. A transaction cannot be reversed, edited, erased, or manipulated; in fact, it is unfeasible at this time and as time passes Bitcoin and the Bitcoin blockchain infrastructure is being developed, secured, and implemented more and more.

So where did Bitcoin come from? Well the cypherpunk community, digital cash developers, and ultimately the developer, Satoshi Nakamoto.

—Cypherpunk: A cypherpunk is any activist advocating widespread use of strong cryptography and privacy-enhancing technologies as a route to social and political change. Cypherpunks have been engaged in an active movement since the late 1980s.

Bitcoin is the collective of ideas bought to a perfect solution and released to the world at the perfect time in history...during the greatest economic recession since the great depression.

Bitcoin.org was registered on August 18, 2008. Soon after a "Peer-to-Peer Electronic Cash System" was published to a mailing list of cryptographers. On January 3, 2009 Satoshi Nakamoto, the founder of Bitcoin mined the first or "genesis block." Satoshi's reward was 50 Bitcoins and in code... embedded in the blockchain was the notation, "The Times 03/Jan/2009 Chancellor on brink of second bailout for banks." This notation refers to an article published by The Times UK, Chancellor Alistair Darling on brink of second bailout for banks. Due to evidence that the 37 billion pound investment earlier the year before failed to keep credit flowing to consumers.

Furthermore, evidence of the financial instability and loss of trust and consumer skepticism in central banks to manage the peoples' money.

Bitcoin is decentralized meaning no government or central bank can manipulate or control it. It is controlled peer to peer and with utmost privacy and security. Your money is your money and no one else's to spend, borrow from, or duplicate.

Between the launch of Bitcoin in 2009 and 2010, the Bitcoin blockchain was developed and honed in to its current state of operation. Over the years many newspapers, books, and other in investigators have tried to find out who Satoshi Nakamoto is. No one really knows the true identity of Satoshi Nakamoto. The name could refer to a single person, a group, a government, a cooperation, or possible of other unknown origin. Regardless, Satoshi Nakamoto was last heard from in April of 2011, when he made a statement that he had, "moved on to other things."

In 2009, one of the first well known Bitcoin transactions took place when two pizzas were ordered and paid for with 10,000 Bitcoins delivered by Papa John's. The value then was about $20, but the value of 10,000 Bitcoins in January of 2019 is $41,000,000. Wow, those are some expensive pizzas!

Chapter Two

• •

Here is a list of the historical value of Bitcoin: *In general...*
2009: zero
2010: about .10 cents each
2011: $1-2 dollars
2012: $2-13 dollars
2013: $13-1000 dollars
2014: $1000-340 dollars
2015: $200-500 dollars
2016: $450-750 dollars
2017: $750-19,783 dollars
2018: $9,000-3,650 dollars
2019: $4,000 +/-
2140: My hypothesis $12,000,000 each

• •

As you can see Bitcoin has ups and downs just like the stock market, commodities, or other currencies. Its values are spiking and declining in extreme curves compared to other more typical assets but this is because it is new technology. Just like when the Internet was first implemented there were many naysayers and procrastination by most to get involved until it was evident it was extraordinary.

A Bitcoin is caged in deep cryptography until it is fully decrypted and birthed to the world through Bitcoin mining. Bitcoin mining is completed by dedicated computers for the sole purpose of mining the Bitcoin algorithm, which is SHA-256. Bitcoin miners store the blockchain ledger on their hard drives and participate in the worlds blockchain accounting ledger.

Bitcoin miners are rewarded with Bitcoin; in which, they can sell their Bitcoin to the world at its current value which puts

Chapter Two

it into circulation, or they may decide to save it in cold storage unit until a later date, which is what most Bitcoin miners seem to be doing currently because they believe a much higher value will happen as time passes.

I hope this answers most of the hidden attributes of Bitcoin and where it originated. Now let's get further into Bitcoin mining and what it entails.

A beautiful day to capture the aerial pic of the Capital in Olympia, Washington. Inspiration for the Capital cover image.

CHAPTER THREE

THE CRITICAL COMPONENTS OF BITCOIN MINING

It's 2015, and I now have Bitcoin in my mind again. I started paying attention to the market. At the time I didn't think I should invest any money straight up into Bitcoin by buying them with US dollars. My wife and I had just sold our business and bought a new home, so spending money on Bitcoin seemed a little too risky. That would be my second regret about Bitcoin. Boy, what a mistake! Had I put any money, borrowed to buy, and sold assets to buy Bitcoin at the time, I could be a multi-millionaire by now. But that's hindsight for yah. It's something I kick myself in the butt about when I think about it, which is why I try not to.

In late 2016, I decided to build a dedicated Bitcoin mining rig. My goal was to get back into mining Bitcoin in the biggest way possible at a residential level. With the price of Bitcoin

Chapter Three

down and without much propulsion many Bitcoin mining farms in the area were going out of business and/or upgrading their equipment. Some Bitcoin mining farms were selling their older miners on eBay, Craigslist, and the like.

I did my research. Trust me, when I decide to make an investment in something, I do all the ground work, studying, and research necessary to ensure a successful end product.

What I learned was that you cannot mine Bitcoin from a gaming computer anymore, that you had to have dedicated Bitcoin miners called ASIC miners running the SHA-256 Cryptographic Hash Algorithm.

What I learned...

#1 Bitcoin miners need power. (Increase in electricity bill)

#2 Bitcoin miners run hot. (Need cooling)

#3 Bitcoin miners are loud. (Cannot be in the house or my wife will kill me)

#1: Power!

Most Bitcoin mining equipment can be run with 110-volt or 220-volt wiring. With 220 volts being safer, slightly more efficient and profitable, I decided to build my rig to run on 220-volt power.

Keeping both safety and economy in mind I figured out that server farms or databases sold their old servers, network switches, and power distribution units (PDUs) on eBay. And they all run on 220 volts!

I arranged 150 amps of power for my home-based Bitcoin mining operation by having an electrician rewire and take power from a couple wall heaters and a 50-amp welding

Chapter Three

circuit. He rewired to use the empty breaker spots. I acquired five PDUs at 30-amps capacity, each off of eBay. I had watched eBay steadily for weeks and ended up purchasing five Servertec PDUs, basically commercial grade 220-voltpower outlet strips. The cool thing about these database PDUs is that they have many safety features, with internal breakers and intranet capabilities. Plus, they give a digital readout of how many amps of power are being drawn by the miners in real time. The Servertec PDUs were going to work essentially as a secondary breaker system separate from the main breakers in the home panel. An important redundancy in case the main circuit breaker failed.

#2: Heat!

I thought long and hard about it and decided there was no way I could have my Bitcoin mining rig in the house. This was due to noise and heat. I thought about the benefits of free heating in the winter but knew the heat pump would be overworked trying to cool the home during the summer. I decided, based on the negatives, that I would setup my Bitcoin operation in the garage.

After researching how to cool the rig, I discovered that typical window-mounted air conditioners would be huge power suckers and likely have short life spans, due to the necessary constant operation. I thought about installing exhaust fans but decided against this as I didn't want to punch holes in the walls of the garage. I decided to run the largest window mount evaporative cooler, or swamp cooler, I could find. They had them in stock at a great deal at the local Costco store, so I bought one, took it home, and installed it. I also purchased a large floor fan from Harbor Freight just in case I needed to direct heat. I purchased the Compaq six exhaust fan unit to pull heat up and out of my Bitcoin mining rig. (I will fill you in on the Compaq server tower later on in this book when I talk about the server rack).

At the time I didn't know for sure if this cooling setup would work, but that was the design I came up with. In the back of my mind I knew that I could always adapt the system if necessary down the road. I rolled with the punches.

I could picture the Bitcoin miners running, the six top mount exhaust fans expelling the hot air created by the miners. The Harbor Freight floor fan recirculating the air in the garage, and the larger evaporative cooler running 24/7, pushing cooled air into the garage interior space. Glorious!

Now at the same time I was building my Bitcoin mining operation, my Cuban friend, we'll call him Pedro, also built a home-based mining operation similar to mine but he installed it in his house, relying on the home's heat pump for cooling. Within about a month of mining, his heat pump died a horrible death and had to be replaced at a cost of about $6000. A very expensive lesson learned about having a Bitcoin mining operation cooled by the home's heat pump. Following my lead, Pedro ended up moving his mining operation to the garage.

I would say that cooling the garage-based mining operation is the most difficult aspect of Bitcoin mining. The good news is, my design using a large window-mounted evaporative cooler works just fine all year round, and I did not have to punch any holes in the walls. I definitely appreciate the heated garage in the cold fall, winter, and spring months of the year.

Of note, I open the garage doors and windows for about 10 minutes during the hottest summer months. This allows all the built-up hot air to be exchanged with the cooler evening air. Another note, our garage attic has a ridge venting setup, which is poor at allowing hot air to escape. To fix the issue I plan to install a powered attic fan and/or a couple solar-powered roof vents with exhaust fans.

Chapter Three

On a fun note, during the hot, dry summer months the kids enjoy swimming in the pool. When they are done swimming and cold to the bone with goose bumps galore, they love standing behind the Bitcoin miners and getting blow dried with hot dry air. With their hair flying back, the goose bumps disappear quickly, and water drops evaporate into the air. Smiles aplenty!

#3 Noise
••••••••••••••••••••••••

Thank God I decided to put this mining operation in the garage! Wow, it is quite impressive how loud it is. I call the high-decibel noise amassed in the garage the sound of money. My wife calls it obnoxious and annoying. But when it is all said and done, the mining operation is loud in the garage and cannot be heard in the house. A mild humming noise can be heard from outside the garage with the garage doors closed, like the hum of a refrigerator compressor running.

So there you have it, the critical components of Bitcoin mining: power, heat, and noise.

••••••••••••••••••••••••

Inside the Compaq Tower looking up at exhaust fans and 3 Antminer S9s.

4-220 volt and 1-110 volt 30 amp plugs.

CHAPTER FOUR

HOW TO BUILD A BITCOIN MINING OPERATION

So how did I successfully build a home-based Bitcoin mining operation? Well it all started when my friend Pedro and I located some Compaq server towers for sale on Craigslist for $150 each. Take in mind, these type of server towers originally cost in the thousands of dollars. They are used in data centers, hospitals, corporations, and other commercial purposes. Not usually found in someone's home! Just like Hillary Clinton, I was about to have my own personal server at home. Watch out Seattle, here we come!

After work on a Wednesday, Pedro and I jumped in my truck and headed to Seattle. We were to meet the seller of the server towers at a shutdown business center.

During the three-hour drive Pedro and I were very excited

and talking about how we were individually going to setup our home-based Bitcoin mining operations. We went on and on about how much money we were about to start making. Bitcoin will have a million-dollar value someday!" said Pedro. This whole process was very fun and memorable.

As the GPS called out directions, Turn right, and You have arrived at your destination, we pulled into a large vacant parking lot at what looked to be a deserted business center. Another remnant of the financial recession. We parked and waited ten minutes and then a Ford Expedition pulled into the parking lot. "Hi guys, I'm Frank," the driver said. "You here for the server towers?"

"Yup!" we said. Frank invited us into the building with him to check out the server racks. As he opened the main doors, we could see that this large facility was indeed vacated. We followed him into the building and down a hall, then boom! There they were. The server towers, all five of them. Two black and three white. What a beautiful sight! We felt their cold metal shells and squeezed all the stainless thumb latches and door mechanisms, testing for faults.

Instantly we could see these were high-quality items, commercial, and built heavy duty. They came with some PDUs pre-installed, Ethernet boards, and shelving racks. There were no negotiations on the price. "We'll take them!" Pedro and I said together. Pedro picked out a tall black one made by Dell, and I picked out a nice clean white one made by Compaq. I chose the white one because I figured it would match the white walls of my garage.

Loading these suckers up into my truck was quite a chore. If you didn't know (and we certainly didn't know until the time), server towers weigh three to four hundred pounds each. "Well worth their weight in Bitcoin I'm sure!" said Pedro. It took Pedro and I to the brink of muscular strain to tip these suckers on their sides onto the tail gate of my truck. We had

Chapter Four

laid cardboard slabs down to protect the towers from the bed of the truck.

Once the towers were tipped and leaning on the tail gate, we then gave them a heave ho and lifted the bases up in the air. We slid them into the bed of the truck. Both server racks were lying on their sides longwise in my eight-foot truck bed with no room to spare. We strapped them down for the four-hour drive home. "Let's get these babies home" I yelled to Pedro as started getting in the driver's side door of my truck. "Time to get rich" Pedro said with a grin and on the road to home we went.

Talk about happy times! Our return trip was spent thinking, talking, and dreaming of all the money we would be making with our Bitcoin mining operations. The feeling was comparable to that hopeful and anticipatory sensational person gets holding on to unscratched lottery ticket. Lucky for Life was our Bitcoin mining scratch card. But at the time of the trip, we had yet to figure out if we had winning tickets or not.

We finally arrived home at about 12:30 a.m. that night. We stopped at my house first to unload my tower and push it into the garage. I then drove Pedro home and unloaded his tower into his driveway.

Pedro planned to setup his mining operation in the basement of his house. So, he had to disassemble the rack and reassemble it inside. It was about one in the morning then and we just wanted to go to bed, so Pedro planned to disassemble his tower the next day. All smiles, we gave each other a fist bump and two thumbs up and then we headed our separate directions. I headed back home and hit the sack as I had to wake up soon and be to work by 6 a.m.

Where to locate your Bitcoin mining operation is likely the most crucial beginning decision. You need to find a location that has power available, won't be too noisy, and has some method to allow heat to escape and or cooling.

Chapter Four

I decided to setup my operation next to the electrical panel in the garage. Luckily the previous owner of our home had installed a fifty amp outlet and circuit for a welder and another four 30-amp breakers for wall heaters. Well, I didn't own a welder, and once my Bitcoin mining operation was up and running, I'd never need heaters in the garage again. So, by taking the welding and wall heater circuits and rewiring them, I was able to pull 150 to 170 amps to for Bitcoin mining.

I decided to have an electrician do all of the work of rewiring the circuits and installing five 30-amp outlets at 220 volts. I didn't want to do the work myself and risk burning down the house. Having a professional electrician do the work will ensure that there won't be any power disruptions, malfunctions, or mistakes. Since I was going to be running all this heat generating equipment in my garage, which is attached to our house, then I want to be able to sleep at night knowing that all safety protocols have been put in place.

I called the electrician and placed the work order. They setup the permit with the Public Utilities District (PUD) and in two weeks I had four 30-amp 220-volt outlets and an extra 30-amp 110-volt one for all the non-220-volt accessories. One hundred and fifty amps of power! Nice. Now all I needed was Bitcoin miners.

Well, not yet. We'll get to them.

Cooling

• •

Now that I had established power, it was time to get a cooling system in place. For one, a nice feature of locating the Bitcoin miners in the garage was that the garage doors could be opened up to allow heat to escape. But I needed a cooling mechanism when the doors were closed. I had contemplated punching a hole in the wall or installing an AC unit, but decided against that because of the amount of power it would cost to run an AC unit 24 hours, a day 7 days a week. I thought about installing a heat pump, but again this would be very costly to install and would likely not last long running at such a capacity (as Pedro learned the hard way). I ultimately decided on a large window-mounted swamp cooler. The power consumption is minimal compared to AC units and will endure long term use.

The model of evaporative cooler I decided on was actually for sale at Costco, the Mastercool MCP 44. Its a large unit that has the option to run the fan only at slow, medium, or high speed and also the option to run the fan and water pump. With the fan on high speed and the pump on this sucker really works well cooling the air in the garage.

Obtaining Bitcoin Miners

Now I needed some Bitcoin miners. Bitcoin miners are computers dedicated to mining Bitcoin. At the time Bitcoin miners were getting easier to purchase, as one of the largest and most popular Bitcoin miner manufactures, Spondoolies, had just gone out of business. Spondoolies was a company in Israel. Prior to going out of business the equipment was very expensive and hard to obtain.

When Spondoolies went out of business Bitcoin mining operators started to liquidate their Spondoolies mining equipment because the technical support was no longer available. I happened to live in the Bitcoin capital of the world, so large scale mining operations within driving distance were selling off their Spondoolies, advertising the Bitcoin miners for sale on Craigslist and eBay.

I ended up calling on a Craigslist ad that had over fifty Spondoolies models SP31 for sale in Quincy, WA. Home of some of the US's largest Yahoo and Microsoft databases and

Chapter Four

only a twenty-minute drive away. I purchased 7 Spondoolies SP31s from this Quincy-based large-scale mining operation. The price was $500 each. That was down from a retail price of $3000 each plus international shipping, so what a bargain!

I purchased three more Spondoolies from a young twenty-something clean-cut Chinese guy in Entiat, WA (about another twenty-minute drive away). His name was Liu Xiang and he talked up Bitcoin like a traveling salesman. He said, "I want to help as many people as I can along the way because the more people that mine Bitcoin the stronger the presence of Bitcoin will become."

He showed Pedro and I the mining rigs, saying, "The more Bitcoin miners in the world the stronger and more powerful the Bitcoin network." Liu Xian was an interesting guy. He drove a nice new BMW convertible, which he pulled into Pedro's driveway in order to sell us some Spondoolies. He told us his home was actually in China, but that he had been living in the US while running and managing a bunch of mining operations in eastern Washington and New York. He was unwilling let me see one of his mining operations due to secrecy and maintaining security, but described them to me as empty warehouses. He had rented and upgraded the power handling capacity for his Bitcoin mining operations. He said that one of his warehouses was at the time going through a PUD upgrade to one megawatt power capacity. That's an insane amount of power consumption! We tested out the Spondoolies in my friend Pedro's living room. We hooked them to a laptop monitoring the mining function and all was in good order. The purchase took place and Liu Xiang was on his way. Keep in mind that at this time, Bitcoin was not yet in the public eye, or news as it is presently. The price of Bitcoin miners was down but about to go astronomical. Now I had a total of ten Spondoolies SP31s ready to setup and put to work! The Spondoolies SP31 is a thing of beauty for sure. I was

Chapter Four

surprised to see how big and heavy each one is. They are made of high-quality server materials and designed to be mounted in server rack towers.

Server Rack Setup

Now that I had my Compaq server tower and cooling system in place, I needed to prepare the server tower. I needed to start purchasing all the necessary server rack shelves for the miners to rest on inside the server tower. I found the best deal on eBay and ordered 12 server rack shelves with all the necessary rack-specific hardware. The hardware is server rack specific (rack screws, nylon washers, and nuts) designed specifically for shelving, servers, or network switches. I ordered 10 shelving setups for the 10 Spondoolies and 2 extras for a server computer and a network switch. The shelving and hardware arrived promptly and as described.

Bitcoin miners need a computer to manage and hold a Bitcoin wallet and run the Bitcoin mining program. I decided to purchase a used Dell PowerEdge 2950 server off eBay. It also arrived fast and as described. I decided on a commercial grade server as I could run it on 220 volts for more power efficiency. You can use pretty much any computer or laptop that has Internet, a large enough hard drive, can run at a high temperature non-stop, and with many failsafe mechanisms in place. For the computer to communicate with all the miners a network switch, or hub, is necessary.

Network Switch

A network switch is a computer networking device that connects devices together on a computer network in addition to the ports on a router. A network switch is necessary because most routers only have 3-6 extra Ethernet Internet outputs and for a Bitcoin mining operation much more Internet connections are needed. I decided on a 48-channel network switch designed for server database use that runs on 220 volts. The model was a Cisco Blade. I purchased it off eBay and it arrived fast and as described, in good working order. To connect the network switch to the computer/or server we need Ethernet cables.

Cat 7/Ethernet Cables

For the computer to receive Internet and communicate to the network switch, which then communicates with each Bitcoin miner, you need Ethernet cables (sometimes called patch cables). I decided on the best quality at the time, which was the Cat 7 gold-plated and shielded cables. I found the best deal on eBay from a seller in China. I ordered enough for all the miners, server, network switch, and extras (if necessary for additions or replacements). I also ordered two one-hundred foot high-quality Cat 7 gold-plated and shielded, one to run from the main provider Internet service, and another from the home's router to the garage mining operation. Now, just as we needed Ethernet cables to connect everything together, we also need to connect all the miners, server, switch, and fans to power.

Power Supply Units (PSUs)

Bitcoin miners need to be powered and my Spondoolies SP31s had 2 PSUs each, which each require a 220-volt power cord. That's a total of twenty 220-volt cords and outlets just to power the ten Spondoolies. The Dell server also had two 220-volt PSUs requiring 2 cords and outlets. The Cisco Blade 48-channel network switch also had two 220-volt PSUs, requiring two cables and outlets. That's a total of twenty-four220-voltPSUs needing 24 heavy duty 220-volt power cords and twenty-four 220-volt outlets to plug them all into. Additional outlets may be necessary for additional servers, server rack cooling fans, or other accessories down the road.

So how do you make available this many 220-volt outlets? Well, you need outlet strips like the ones you use for your TV entertainment system or computer work station at home. However commercial database servers, Bitcoin miners, and database equipment require much more sophisticated and heavy-duty version of standard outlet strips called PDUs.

Power Distribution Units (PDUs)

Database or server farm PDUs are 220 volts and provide a digital readout for amp draw or real time power consumption. These also communicate with the server or computer via the Internet. From the server or computer, you can see the power draw and power performance of each individual outlet which corresponds to the Bitcoin miner, server, or switch plugged into it. They also have much heavier wiring and casing to handle hotter temperatures and increase protection from wear and tear.

For my Bitcoin mining operation, I ordered four Server Technology Sentry (which means they supply Branch Circuit Protection) PDUs at thirty amps each. Called Servertech for short, this PDU has more than enough outlets. I just needed to make sure I distributed the miners evenly between the PDUs to not overload them. I also purchased one 30-amp 110-volt Compaq PDU to provide outlets for all the 110-volt equipment and accessories. That's a total of five commercial grade PDUs, four Servertech PDUs, and one Compaq 110-volt PDU. Now to plug them all in...But wait! PDUs and miners do not come with power cables or plug ins to connect them to the PDUs. Let's take another step.

Power Cables
●●●●●●●●●●●●●●●●●●●●●●●●●

Bitcoin miners usually do not come with power cords. They are a separate item that I found best obtained from eBay, as they are expensive. The power cables necessary to plug my Spondoolies, Dell server, and Blade network switch into the Servertech PDUs are heavy-duty C14 to C13 power cables. Make sure to get the heavy duty cables for best power efficiency and safety. Now that all the equipment is able to communicate via Ethernet cables, and power up via the power distribution units, we need to turn things on. But wait again! FYI, servers don't come with an operating system like Windows or Macintosh. They are blank and waiting for an operating system to be installed.

Operating System (OS)
●●●●●●●●●●●●●●●●●●●●●●●●●

The Dell server I purchased came without an operating system. (A wiped hard drive, just like my poor red Viper, no doubt.) I contemplated using either a Linux, Windows, Macintosh, or Android. I ultimately decided on installing a professional version of Windows Server 2012 R2 Data Center. I purchased the operating system off of eBay and installed it, no problem.

Chapter Four

Internet Service Provider (ISP)
••••••••••••••••••••••••

When it comes to Bitcoin mining from home don t go with slow Internet service. I recommend having the fastest possible Internet service available to your home. Fiber optic and cable are fast, but what matters most is what package you purchase from your ISP. The more gigs of bandwidth or data streaming the better. This typically translates to "the more you pay, the better the service." I have the fastest service possible in my area. Using an app called *SPEEDCHECK* Speed Test, I clocked my Internet speed and the results were as follows:

Ping = 40ms
Download = 137.62 Mbps
Upload = 191.84 Mbps

 I believe that the speed listed above is overkill, but my family and I are heavy Internet users. We pay for the best and are able to have this speed due to the well developed fiber, SkyFi by Localtel, and cable network infrastructure in Douglas County. We have no problems running Bitcoin mining, streaming 4K movies, YouTube, TV, and video games simultaneously, along with data-sucking cell phones and tablets within the home. All this with zero glitches or lag time. None. All in use, mining and streaming with no pixilation. It may sound like a lot of simultaneous device use, but this is a typical household situation nowadays.
 The Internet of Things (IOT) is only growing in homes and communities across the globe. The Internet of Things refers to the interconnection of everyday technological devices via the Internet enabling them to connect, interact, and exchange data.

Chapter Four

In 1993 when I was a senior in high school we went on a class trip to Seattle. Our trip was a boat tour on Lake Washington then evening party or graduation celebration. The boat tour took us by Bill Gate's home. I remember how unbelievable the description the tour guide gave about Bill Gate's home seemed. He said that Bill Gates built his home customized with many automation features like voice and facial recognition, smart lights, and sensors. It seemed so unrealistic and unattainable in that time, but now look. Its 2019 and we can talk to "Alexa" or "Hey Google" and automate our homes lighting, air conditioning, plugs, televisions, kitchen appliances, and so much more. If you're not connected your missing out on a fun, unraveling, and exciting time in the history of technology. Get on the bandwagon!

Router

Regardless of Internet service and speed, your home intranet (with a home server running a Bitcoin mining operation off of a network switch allows home based cloud, website, or other interconnectivity between devices within your home Internet system or intranet) and Wi-Fi will vary greatly on the quality of your router. I surveyed the available routers just prior to writing this book and did an upgrade on our router and wow! What a difference in signal power and speed for Wi-Fi uploads and downloads. The router I purchased was the Netgear Nighthawk X10.

According to Internet reviews the Nighthawk X10 AD7200 is the industry's fastest router for media streaming with Plex Media Server. It delivers ultra-smooth 4Kstreaming, seamless virtual reality (VR) gaming, and near instant downloads. When it comes to Bitcoin mining and your Internet you don't want crappy service or a slow router to dam up the flow of Bitcoin

Chapter Four

into your wallet.

You know, it is amazing how nowadays you can buy just about anything you need or desire off the Internet. New or used, buy or sell, even barter is an option with a plethora of online entities like eBay, Craigslist, Amazon, Google, Walmart.com, Hayneedle, etc. How did people function before the Internet? [Oh right. Well, this beats the pants off of The Little Nickel.]

It took me about six months to figure out all of the listed steps, equipment, etc., which is way too long. Beginning to end, gathering the necessary equipment, permits, and install should have only taken a month of two. At the time there were only complicated and poorly detailed blogs and YouTube videos with the details on "how to" setup a home Bitcoin mining operation. The lack of easy to understand and complete information available was one of the driving forces for me to write this book. I want to lay it all out there in easy to understand language to help you all that are seeking to become Bitcoin miners be successful out of the gates.

That just about wraps up the basic necessities for starting your own Bitcoin mining operation. Here is a synopsis of the list, just in case you decide to go all in and become a Bitcoin miner like me.

DIY Bitcoin Mining

#1 Power: You need to make sure you locate your mining operation in a place with enough power to meet your needs. Have a professional electrician do all the wiring and the installation of 220-volt outlets. The electrician should obtain all the necessary permits for your electrical work and mining operation.

#2 Internet: You can't mine Bitcoin without Internet, and you want the fastest, most reliable connection you can attain from your provider. The router you choose should be able to handle mining and all the other non-Bitcoin essentials of the modern home, including 4K streaming, VR gaming, TV, YouTube, Amazon, etc. The best router should be capable of handling all plugged and wireless Internet devices simultaneously.

#3 Computer: I recommend an up-to-date computer with a newer version OS, quality video card, SSD main hard drive, and a newer processor. The computer needs to have Ethernet, USB ports, monitor, keyboard, and mouse to do the job. A used laptop will work just as well, but a newer one will have all the bells and whistles.

#4 Network Distribution Switch or Switches: This depends on how many Bitcoin miners you plan to operate. One network signal comes into your home and it needs to have enough channels to connect via Internet to your computer and miners.

#5 PDUs: Depending on how many Bitcoin miners you plan to operate, each one will need an outlet to plug into. This is accomplished with PDUs. PDUs are heavy duty outlet strips. You will need enough PDUs to provide the same amperage capability as the miners require. The best scenario is to run 220-volt PDUs and 220-volt Bitcoin miners as 220 volt has less chance of overheating and burning up as well as most Bitcoin miners nowadays require 220 volt power sources. 110 volt Bitcoin mining is becoming obsolete.

#6 Racks: You will need some good solid racks for placing Bitcoin miners. They need to be made of metal. Costco has good deals on high quality storage racks that would work just fine for a Bitcoin mining operation. I prefer to use a server

Chapter Four

tower and racks to decrease the amount of space required. The racks need to be made of metal to withstand the heat dispersion that comes from the miners and also for fire prevention.

#7 Bitcoin Miners: Antminer S15, T15, S9s, S9 hydros, or newer versions as they are developed after the writing this book, and as many as you can based on your available power. I started out with used Spondoolies and this worked just fine. Really as long as you're mining, your making money. The newer and higher quality the miner, the more money at the best power efficiency will be achieved.

#8 Accessories: Cat 7 gold-plated Ethernet cables, heavy-duty power cables for miners, switches, and fans, USB memory stick, USB Ledger or Trezor cryptocurrency wallet for cold storage in a safe, a notepad or multiple copies of passcodes, keys, passphrases, etc. This last one is an important redundancy. You really, really don't want to lose your Bitcoin because you forgot the password or lost the private keys.

"Once you have acquired and setup all of the components of Bitcoin mining, turn it on and let's get these babies humming."

• •

Chapter Four

CHAPTER FIVE

HOW TO START MINING FOR BITCOINS

The first time I powered up my PDUs, server, network switch, and Bitcoin miners, I was so excited that I could hardly breath. Oh, how cool to finally hear all the fans turn on. Whoosh! First the computer or server fans, then the network switch, and finally the miners screaming away. All the LEDs blinking on and off during the various startup sequences as the mining operation boots up and comes alive. The building of the mining operation is nothing compared to the sound of the Bitcoin miners.

Soon all the miners are mining at full mining power, called hashing power by miners. The sound is unique and unusual. The miners are humming along loudly with a sort of whining and grinding sound of a wind turbine or small jet engine. This

Chapter Five

noise remains constant and does not vary— neither wax nor wane. "This is the sound of money!" I said to myself, when I first cranked it on. I pictured zillions of little men with pick axes hacking away at the block of code, trying to get the Bitcoins. Just like the dwarfs in Lord of the Rings tunneling through the mountains of Moria pick axes in hand hacking away at a mountain looking for gold.

Did you know gold is alien, as in, not of this earth? It's a fact. It was deposited on earth from meteors of cosmic origins millions of years ago. This is one reason gold is considered valuable. Gold has many uses including as a heavy weight, a conductor of electricity, artwork, and of course as a store of value. That is, money. There is only so much of it and to get it you must buy it or do the work and find it through gold mining.

Bitcoin is like gold. It is rare and limited to 21 million Bitcoins for the whole world to share. It is buyable and minable. It is now tradable like stocks and is a much more efficient means to transfer or exchange value than gold. Can you imagine if you wanted to sell, trade, or pay for something with gold how difficult it would be? Let's say you have a million dollars worth of gold (thats currently 3600 pounds) and you want to use it to pay for something overseas. The transaction would require manual labor moving the gold blocks, a commercial truck, commercial shipping or flight, customs inspection, crossing international borders, and finally local delivery to the gold's final destination. Do you think all 3,600 pounds of gold would arrive intact? Or in this inconvenient process, could some have been stolen? My bet is the entire sum of one million dollars worth of gold would not have made it. The transaction using gold would take forever and is risky compared to using Bitcoin. One million dollars worth of Bitcoin can be transferred securely in a matter of minutes using the Bitcoin network and blockchain technology. No middle man or other entities to skim from your money. No one telling you what you can or can't spend your money on. This is the future.

The future of Bitcoin mining is going to be huge. I plan to have my home based Bitcoin mining operation going on into retirement. I will upgrade the equipment when needed to remain profitable. The extra money will help fund travel, healthcare, or whatever else tickles my fancy. I wrote an entire chapter in this book on retiring and mining Bitcoin.

Bitcoin mining done correctly can be a person's full or part time job. Bitcoin mining as a career seems unrealistic but it is totally possible. You just need to have a good understanding and experience on how Bitcoin, Bitcoin mining, and the economy work. Stay tuned for a little briefing on a Bitcoin mining as a career in the next chapter.

–Here's **simple start-up checklist on how to start mining**, once all necessary equipment is setup, connected, and powered on:

1. Setup Operating System (OS): Enter BIOS and setup power to remain on constant/forever to avoid shutdowns or automatic restarts. (There are many videos on YouTube that guide you through setting up the BIOS for Bitcoin mining. Just put the video on your smart phone and follow along).

2. Download mining wallet: I prefer the Bitcoin Core client @bitcoin.org

3. Plug in miners: They will auto start when plugged in.

4. Find the IP address of each miner: Enter your home router or network@ IP address 192.168.0.1 or 192.168.1.1 You will need the user name and password of your home router to do this.

5. Setup each miner: Enter the mining pool in the correct location. Follow the instructions for setup that comes with your miner. There are also many YouTube videos as resources. I prefer Kano Pool as I can mine anonymously.

6. Direct all mining shares to your Bitcoin core wallet "Receiving Address." Once connected to a pool and your Bitcoin wallet address is setup as the receiving end of all mining shares that's pretty much it. It's automatic from this point on.

7. Keep everything running. Sometimes miners need to be restarted for various reasons. Just simply unplug them in the case of Antminer S9s and Spondoolies, count to ten then plug them back in. They should automatically start mining again. Just go into the miners settings after running for 10 minutes and verify it is still linked to your router. You may need to go into your router settings and search for a new IP as sometimes the miner will get assigned a new one. Then enter that new IP in the web address bar and the control panel for the miner will open up.

8. It's optional but wise to move Bitcoin (BTC) from a computer or online based wallet to an **offline or cold storage wallet** like the Trezor, Nano S, or Ledger Blue.

CHAPTER SIX

BITCOIN MINING AS A CAREER

Talk about a career that is a no-brainer. I mean, no college debt, no years grinding away in college classes, and a lot of free time on your hands. A career as a Bitcoin miner.

I don't want to distract from the base of knowledge and the core of all careers here. Don't get me wrong. Education is key and with it success in life and income earning potential. I'm purely being a bit imaginary and speculative here, which is high risk. Please understand I wrote this chapter based on what I have learned about Bitcoin and the history of tech investment opportunities that have passed like Google, Microsoft, and Amazon. The environment and possibilities that exist currently did not exist when I was young. The opportunities of the present as far as Bitcoin did not exist when I was first earning and working towards my future. Young adults, college grads, working adults, and retirees all have a unique shot at increasing their wealth with Bitcoin mining and investment. I'm talking here about a time in history that needs action fast because the time is now, before Bitcoin mining becomes too regulated, difficult, and expensive for the average Joe to participate. Bitcoin is in a start-up company phase of development per se. Like investing in Microsoft, Google, and Amazon in the early stages when it was speculative and risky. Don't you wish you had or could have had the opportunity to invest in those rich companies in the early development stages when they were cheap? Investments in those companies have paid off far better for early investors compared to the present status quo. I'm after the fast money.

The sudden yet risky chances at massive wealth. Before I'm dead. "One life" as Gary Vaynerchuck says. How you going down? A risk taker or a buttoned-up ultraconservative playing it safe in all your movements. Whatever choices you make I am in full respect. That is the cool thing about this life. Freedom of choice. Free will you might say. It takes all variations to make the world the amazing thing it is today.

Please take my high risk ideas with a grain of salt and with much gravity at the same time. I mean everything I say. To become a Bitcoin miner takes money. You need money to buy the equipment, possibly rent a warehouse -vs- home based mining operation. So apparently you must have money on hand to pave your path. Bitcoin mining is an investment. Do you have money from your parents to go to college? A trust fund directed towards your future? Do you need to work awhile to earn money first to be able to invest in Bitcoin and perhaps Bitcoin mining? Are you already post college in a career looking for additional income or maybe want to take a risk on a possible Microsoft type (or bigger even) investment in the early stages? A retiree wanting added income streams and Bitcoin mining is on your radar? Whatsoever your situation you're reading this book and I am the dramatist, the abstractor, the framer for

Chapter Six

what I believe in and that is that Bitcoin is going to change the world and spawn many other technological breakthroughs. Bitcoin is going to be bigger than any tech investment we as a world economy have ever lived through to date.

That being said the average college-goers spends two to seven years attending to and learning what is necessary for their dream job. Imagine if you took those two to seven years and traded that time in for a career in Bitcoin mining. Don't get me wrong, college is a great experience and an education is an incredible asset. But man, what if you took all that college money and at eighteen or nineteen years old rent a shop, acquire 480 amps of power, setup 48 Antminer S9 miners, and from that point just maintain the operation! Or, even better, attend college on the side! At current Bitcoin value ($3,900 in the winter of 2019), that is about a 16-Bitcoin-a-year income or $62,400 a year, minus about $16,800 in power cost. That is a total of $45,600 a year profit.

That's more income in the first year than most college jobs. Now imagine if the value of Bitcoin goes up over time, which is what most Bitcoin enthusiast believe and why they are all in. Let's go back to December of 2017, when Bitcoin value rose to just over $19,000. At that value the first years income would be $304,000, minus the $16,800 power expense, giving us a total profit of $287,200 a year income. Now that's money in the bank! So, what if the future value of Bitcoin rises to $50,000?

Of course, there are some things to consider, like living expenses. Let's say living expenses are $40,000 a year, which is living pretty sweet for a young adult. At an income of $62,400 that still leaves you a decent amount of Bitcoin earnings each year to save in your Bitcoin wallet.

Half your Bitcoin saved at current hashing difficulty and Bitcoin value is 8 to 10 Bitcoins saved. That's $31,200 to $39,000 dollars, based on the January 2019 Bitcoin value of about $3,900. Now, what if the value of Bitcoin in the year 2020 rises to $50,000? Well, these Bitcoins you saved are now worth $400,000 to $500,000. If you take that into consideration, in your first year you mined 16 Bitcoins, spent 6 to 8 on living expenses, and saved the other 8 to 10 Bitcoins. That's a $540,000 income for the first year of Bitcoin mining! Aside from the possible exponential income growth there is a lot of free time on a Bitcoin miner's hands. To maintain 48 Bitcoin miners is simply just observing them once and awhile to check that they are all hashing and infrequently need to be powered down and reset or repaired.

Well, how many careers require zero college and only about 30 minutes a day labor for a potentially lucrative income? I don't know of any others. This allows a Bitcoin miner to get a second job, full or part time to make more money and have a safety net in the ebbs and flows of the Bitcoin mining protocol and value fluctuations. Or go on lots of leisurely hikes, embrace recreation, play video games, whatever toots your horn!

As a career Bitcoin miner, you will likely want to scale your operation over time. I mean, why have 48 Antminers when you can have 480 Antminers? Why have a shop when you can have an airport hangar? Why not consider making Bitcoin mining a career? Risk? Failure? All career choices have risks as well as positive and negative attributes depending on the economy, culture, and other variables. Bitcoin mining is no different.

I want you to keep one thing on your mind as I and all Bitcoin miners of the earth also do and that is that the difficulty of mining Bitcoin, the hash algorithm, is increasing or becoming more difficult as time passes. Therefore all the numbers I have listed are based on the mining difficulty and hash algorithm as it is at the time of writing this book. As a Bitcoin miner, I am aware of the current mining difficulty, profit, and know that down the road I will need to replace or upgrade all my Bitcoin operation with newer, more efficient, higher producing Bitcoin miners. "I'm waiting Samsung!"

To give you an example of my personal operation I am running twelve S9's at 168 TH and in June of 2018 was earning over $2300 a month Bitcoin value and in the late fall of 2018 the same mining operation $900 a month, and in January 2019 $585 Bitcoin income. The numbers are fluctuating due to the value of Bitcoin in the spring of 2018 being about $9000 a Bitcoin and in the late fall a $5,300 a Bitcoin and in January 2019 a $3,900 Bitcoin. So my monthly mining income is down because of a twofold situation. One, the mining difficulty is harder than in the spring, and two the value of Bitcoin I mine is down purely due to a downturn in the Bitcoin market.

I have zero worry. Zero anxiety about lowering Bitcoin value. I see it as an opportunity to get in before it goes viral again. As a Bitcoin miner I just want Bitcoin. I want it in my wallet and I want it to stay. I personally am a long term investor in Bitcoin. I believe the value will be astronomical in years to come and I will cash out at that time...maybe.

Chapter Six

Bitmain Antminer S9 and Power Supply Unit (PSU)

Mastercool Evaporative Cooler. Low cost cooling year round.

CHAPTER SEVEN

THE BITCOIN CAPITAL OF THE WORLD

Douglas County in Washington state, USA, is the place to be for Bitcoin mining. Douglas County now earns the title of Bitcoin Capital of the World. The Bitcoin industry is not the first to discover Douglas County though. In the last eight to ten years Yahoo, Microsoft, and other large entities have been setting up humungous data centers around here. The reason is the abundant and affordable power. Douglas County is surrounded by hydroelectric, solar, and wind power sources. Central Washington residents have enjoyed some of the cheapest power in the world at $.023/Kilowatt Hour(KWH) first 25,000 KWH.

Douglas County also has a great Internet infrastructure because of a massive investment in fiber optic technology. Most

Chapter Seven

cities in Douglas County have fiber optic data lines, which are working their fingers into the county countryside.

Douglas County is primarily agricultural and there is an abundance of land available. Douglas County, at the time of writing this book, is Bitcoin mining friendly. There are so many large and small mining entities trying to get established here that Douglas County Public Utilities District (PUD) has had to ramp up staffing and processes to handle customer service. Other areas in central Washington are also enjoying the influx of business.

Bitmain, one of the most powerful Bitcoin entities in the world has established roots in East Wenatchee, Douglas County and Walla Walla Washington, as well as 16 other areas of the USA.

In the Spring of 2018 the US government, Washington state, and counties all paved the way for a China born company to establish roots and do business in America. Bitmain is the largest manufacture of Bitcoin miners and equipment in the world.

This is a monumental move in the cryptocurrency world and represents big things to come. The Bitmain-owned company Ant Creek was flying under the radar until recently released news in the spring of 2018. The Bitmain owned mining database in Douglas county wasn't even known until the day of the ribbon cutting ceremony in November of 2018. You have to admit that it's a sign of the future if the world's largest manufacturer of cryptocurrency miners decides, of all places in the entire US of A, to establish its first roots in central Washington.

This says a lot about central Washington. You know that this company did its due diligence and thorough research before deciding where to establish operations in the USA. Central Washington state, especially Douglas County, has a solid infrastructure of power generation and distribution, cheap

Chapter Seven

land, and is cryptocurrency friendly. Given the facts, Bitmain's move to Central Washington makes total sense.

Within Douglas County lies the city of East Wenatchee. East Wenatchee sits on the Columbia River, on the border of wheat land and apple orchards. From East Wenatchee east across Washington state (about three and a half hours of driving) is mostly agricultural land and of that canola, hay, and wheat farming. If irrigated...then wine vineyards, apple orchards, corn, beans, etc. From the Columbia river extending east across the state to Spokane is all considered eastern Washington. Eastern Washington is a beautiful mix of mountains, rivers, lakes, and open country. The price of real estate in eastern Washington is on, and has been on for over a decade, an exponential and meteoric rise in value. The jig is up. The word is out. It seems like people from all over the county are uprooting and making the move to eastern Washington.

You cannot go wrong investing in eastern Washington real estate, especially in the Wenatchee area. It seems to only appreciate in value, year after year. Not only is there beautiful land as far as the eye can see, there's also some of the cheapest power in the world, real estate appreciation, and high-quality health care.

Confluence Health services most of central Washington and can provide all the medical and surgical services necessary to provide for a stable retirement or family relocation.

When a person is coming close to retiring they should be thinking of relocating to an area that has great health care. That's one of the reasons that Chelan and Douglas counties have some of the highest real estate appreciation in the country. There are many retirees selling their homes in California and Seattle moving to a beautiful area with endless outdoor activities.

Tourist destinations like Leavenworth and Lake Chelan are only twenty minutes away. Great healthcare is right in the

Chapter Seven

heart of Wenatchee. No more sitting in hours of congested traffic on the California and Seattle highways, and real estate at a fraction of the cost. This all leaves retirees with plenty of money in the bank and plenty of time to enjoy it.

There is an airport in East Wenatchee called Pangborn, which is central to many Bitcoin mining farms and data centers. There is much land available surrounding the airport, but it is getting swallowed up quickly by the tech industry, big companies, and developers.

Pangborn has flights to Seattle and Spokane. This makes it convenient for big tech moguls, investment tycoons, and foreign interests to bounce in and out as they need to monitor their Bitcoin investments. Everybody has to keep an eye on their money.

The Life Here

I have lived most of my life in the Wenatchee Valley. I have witnessed firsthand the Apple Capital of the World slowly morph out of apples and into wineries, Bitcoin and retirement. A place where retirees enjoy great healthcare, low traffic, outdoor recreations galore, and live off their Bitcoin mining operations, humming along in their garages! It's fine living here.

All joking aside, there has been much news on Bitcoin mining in the local newspaper, The Wenatchee World. The news dealing with Bitcoin in spring of 2018 is mostly about individuals exercising their right to plug something in to the power they are paying for. There are hundreds if not thousands of people running varying sizes of Bitcoin miners in their homes, garages, shops, outbuildings, sheds, and shipping containers. Most of the news is centered around speculation by the PUD, anti-Bitcoin mining individuals, and other residents

Chapter Seven

who are worried about the cost of power rising rapidly due to demand for power by Bitcoin mining entities. It's actually quite a spectacle.

The city of Wenatchee and Chelan County have put a moratorium on Bitcoin mining and are penalizing individuals with steep fines, even threatening to shut off people s electricity. For one, central Washington has so much of an overabundance of power that it sells most of it to California and Seattle. It's funny to me how the local Wenatchee government and Chelan County PUD are focusing on the small Bitcoin mining operations. Imagine going after a retired doctor with a couple Bitcoin miners in the garage, using his or her power and paying for it. It's no different from using a home computer to host a website, for social media marketing or computer gaming, or running a home server or cloud, and other freedoms of life. No fines as yet for hot tubs, heated pools, or shop welders! These things use massive amounts of power and are not penalized, ticketed, threatened, or harassed about.

There is an overabundance of power available in central Washington and it doesn't make financial sense to pick on the little guy, the individual home owner plugging in a few miners. When you consider that large scale Bitcoin mining operators are bringing in millions of dollars to build up the infrastructure it only makes sense to open the doors and monetize in this rising technology. Of note recently Chelan county announced and up and coming regulation and fee schedule. My advise, do your Bitcoin mining business in Douglas county, a Bitcoin friendly establishment.

If you take every single one of the individual small entities running Bitcoin mining equipment, combine them together, and compare the sum to a large entity like Bitmain, Giga Watt, or Salcido Enterprises. Well, there is no comparison. The amount of power consumption is insignificant to the big dogs, let alone all the combined hot tubs, heated pools, and welding stations in the area. The personal home-based Bitcoin coin miners are a drop in the bucket, insignificant in the grand scheme of power consumption, and should be left alone.

If the Chelan county PUD continues to fine its paying customers and to threaten shutting off their home power, they are going to be slapped with a large class action lawsuit. To me it is un-American and wrong to punish an innocent person for using electricity that they pay for to do something with it that is totally legal, not hurting anybody, and a possibly at earning a better quality of life financially. Just like a gold miner mining for gold, there needs to be a legal not illegal path for all to enjoy their right to mine the worldwide Internet phenomenon that is Bitcoin.

Regardless of the local news and the Chelan county PUD debacle, this area of the country is beautiful, rewarding, and a premium location to setup roots. People from all over the world are moving to the Pacific Northwest and not moving away. The secret or unknown benefits of living in the Pacific Northwest, specifically eastern Washington, is a cat-out-of-the-bag scenario. Eastern Washington enjoys the best of all four seasons with an early spring, long summer days, beautiful fall weather, and winters mild, yet snowy where it counts.

A person can enjoy every outdoor adventure known to man, all within a thirty-minute drive. The list of abundant opportunities include hiking, camping, canoeing, kayaking, river rafting, water skiing, boating, jet skiing, rock climbing, scuba diving, road biking, mountain biking, leisure bicycling, scenic drives, all-terrain vehicle (ATV) and motorcycle trail riding, hunting, fishing, precious metal and gem mining, metal detecting, snow shoeing, snow skiing, snowboarding, snow racing, snowmobiling, cross country skiing, marathons, festivals, fairs, parades, carnivals, hot springs, bed and breakfasts, outdoor gyms, public playgrounds, water parks, dog parks, an old western themed town (Cashmere and Winthrop,

Chapter Seven

WA), a Bavarian/German theme tourist town (Leavenworth, WA), honey hiving, chicken cooping, trail riding, horseback riding, back country horsemen, the Enchantments, Cascades, waterfalls, lakes, rivers, ponds, national forests, and many more not listed all in fair weather conditions with no traffic jams, cheap power, and life in the American dream.

Eastern Washington has to be one of the best locations on earth to work, raise a family, retire, and enjoy all life has to offer. I can't imagine living anywhere else it's so nice. Especially considering the repeating news about the terrible conditions of the Midwest, Southwest, and the East Coast. Hurricanes, tornadoes, droughts, flooding, severe northeastern winters, ice storms, swamps and alligators in the south, extended and sometimes severe dry heat in the Southwest, the smog and traffic congestion, high cost of living, and high crime rates in big cities.

The list goes on, but you get the point. There's not much to complain about in eastern Washington except maybe wind and, along with it, allergies. Well, there is the recent hazard caused from wildfires that have stricken the west coast from southern California to the Pacific Northwest. There is a benefit and a cost to every living location. Weigh your options and pick your poison...or delight.

So, if life sucks where you live, if the weather is uncomfortable, if the land is ugly, if there is little to do and you need a change for the great, then consider a move here to Douglas County, in the heart of Central Washington, *The Bitcoin Capital of the World.*

Where the Bitcoin flows from the power lines like honey from a hive.

Central/Eastern Washington is the new retirement Mecca of the USA, great place to raise a family and live out your dream career. Come and enjoy job growth and upper-end salaries, rapid real estate appreciation, and abundant recreation. Thrive in the beauty of all four seasons, mild weather, and some of the highest count of sunny days in America. Live in the aura of health and wellness, good eats, exercise, and active lifestyles. Be secure knowing some of the finest physicians, therapists, and nurses are present in a full-service and state-of-the-art health care environment ready to serve you and your retirement or family needs. Celebrate at the plethora of wineries, breweries, and festivals that take place throughout the year. Come to central Washington and live out the American dream!

Work, live, and retire mining Bitcoin. In the Bitcoin Capital of the World...

...and if you ever come to visit the Bitcoin capital of the world. In the conclusion of this book I have included a list or checklist of the things you need to see here. A roadmap of destinations you must visit... John Van Leyden's personal tour centered around the Bitcoin Capital of The World.

CHAPTER EIGHT

KEEP YOUR FINGER ON THE PULSE

Everybody wishes they would have invested in startup years of Microsoft, IBM, Apple, Amazon, or Google. Well, one thing about technology is that it is constantly evolving. As soon as a technology is thriving, boom!...another technological breakthrough makes the prior obsolete. Bitcoin is the technological breakthrough for the financial and banking system. The current financial system is still using material money, a technology dating back to Mesopotamia, circa 3000 B.C. Bitcoin and the blockchain are going to blow the walls off our current prehistoric banking environment. This could possibly lead to the end of banks as we know them, but that's a topic for another day.

Here are some companies, ideas, and technologies that I feel

Chapter Eight

are worth monitoring.

First? Anything Winklevoss twins. Why? Because they have their fingers on the pulse of Bitcoin technology, especially dealing with exchange-traded funds (ETFs), security, and storage. The Winklevoss twins were paid a settlement of $65,000,000 in a lawsuit against Mark Zuckerberg, owner of Facebook (en.wikipedia.org/wiki/Winklevoss_twins). Let's stay focused on what the Winklevoss twins have to do with Bitcoin. They invested a large portion of their Facebook settlement into buying straight up Bitcoin. Eleven million dollars worth.

In March of 2013, the Winklevoss twins purchased 100,000 Bitcoins at a value of about $120 each. Their eleven-million-dollar investment in 2013 made them billionaires by 2017. By investing in Bitcoin, they made a billion dollars in four years. At the highest point (December of 2017) they had $1.9 billion in Bitcoin, nearly 2 billion from an 11-million-dollar investment. As I'm writing this book in the fall of 2018 and on into 2019, the value of Bitcoin is fluctuating between four and seven thousand dollars and their 100,000 Bitcoins are worth about $700 million. They have lost a significant amount since Bitcoin's rally in December of 2017, but still an impressive investment. A little bit of a sting going from 1.9 billion to 700 million in less than a year…but remember, only a 11 million dollar investment. Still a great return on investment for the Winklevoss Twins.

As visionaries in Bitcoin technology, I know the Winklevoss twins are not worried about it the fluctuations in Bitcoin value at this time. If anything they are likely taking advantage of the low pricing and making more Bitcoin investments. In fact, I bet they remain very excited about the future of Bitcoin. As all Bitcoin believers know, the value of Bitcoin 20 to 30 years from now will be astronomical compared to what we are seeing now. Tim Draper an American venture capitalist, and

Chapter Eight

founder of Draper University recently tweeted his predication of a Bitcoin value of $250,000 by 2022. The numbers are all over the place when it comes to the upper echelons speculative hypothesis but all are mapping Bitcoin value to soar to massive high value as the infrastructure and use of Bitcoin increases around the world over time. Imagine a day when Bitcoin is worth around $225,000 or more each. When and if this happens, the Winklevoss twins 11-million-dollar investment will be worth 22 billion 500 million dollars. Not bad. Not bad at all.

The Winklevoss twins are working behind the scenes on digital and cryptocurrency technology. They also own and operate the Gemini Exchange, "The Bridge to the Future of Money." The Gemini Exchange is a next generation digital asset exchange and custodian where you can purchase, sell, and store digital assets in a regulated, secure, and compliant manner. The Gemini Exchange headquarters is located in New York City, is a New York trust company regulated by the New York State Department of Financial Services. The Gemini Exchange hosts Bitcoin, Bitcoin Cash, Litecoin, Ethereum, and Z-cash. Gemini has also recently issued its own cryptocurrency called Gemini Dollar ticker GUSD said to be the world's first stablecoin.

The Winklevoss twins have also been working with the US government and the Securities and Exchange Commission (SEC) to list a cryptocurrency ETF (Exchange Traded Fund) with the stock ticker COIN on a regulated exchange. The SEC has rejected the application twice as of September of 2018, but the future remains hopeful. Currently as of November 2018 the situation is on standstill as the SEC continues to delay their decision on Bitcoin ETFs.

Another entity to monitor in order to keep your finger on the pulse is Van Eck. Van Eck is a global financial investment management company based in New York City. Van Eck is well known for their "vector" ETFs and currently pushing for Van Eck "Solid X Bitcoin Trust," a cryptocurrency ETF. Van Eck continues just as the Winklevoss twins, to establish the first SEC approved Bitcoin/cryptocurrency ETF.

In December of 2017 the US Government approved futures trading on Bitcoin. In my mind this was a win/lose situation. Win: the US government further acknowledges the presence of Bitcoin and its value. Lose: with the price of Bitcoin rising exponentially it creates an environment of investing against Bitcoin. Add in the hysteria caused by the media, and then speculation, and the sometimes volatile nature of Bitcoin. This environment derailed Bitcoin and its meteoric rise to the top in December of 2017. This is really too bad.

John McAfee, a British-American computer programmer and businessman, founded one of the world's largest software companies, McAfee. The company, McAfee is well known for creating antivirus products and other digital security intelligence. John sold his share of MacAfee and went on to other ventures. John McAfee is now a large-scale investor in Bitcoin technology, Bitcoin mining databases or farms, and is a social media informer. John predicts a $500,000 value of a Bitcoin by the year 2020. He said, "If not, I will eat my own dick on national television." He is a bit controversial yet keeps his finger on the pulse; he's another one to monitor- or not if his voice offends.

Giga Watt (giga-watt.com) is "The world's first full-service specialized computer power provider." Giga Watt is a company located in the Bitcoin Capital of the world, our own Douglas County. Giga Watt is a one stop cryptocurrency mining operation. If you want to become a Bitcoin miner you can bring your machines or purchase Bitcoin miners through Giga Watt, then set them up in their server racks and pay Giga Watt to keep them powered up and running reliably, all for a monthly power and maintenance fee. In this deal, Giga Watt

Chapter Eight

is basically "hosting" your Bitcoin mining operation. All your Bitcoin miners are pointed to your Bitcoin wallet and you can just sit back, pay the bill, and watch your Bitcoin deposits grow. This is a great solution for anyone wanting to own a Bitcoin mining operation outside their home, garage, shop. It's also great if you don't have cheap power or fast Internet in your area. Giga Watt also offers a currency of their own called a Giga Watt token (WTT). This company keeps their fingers on the pulse of cryptocurrencies and Bitcoin and should be monitored.

FYI: Update: Giga Watt just filed for Chapter 11 bankruptcy in mid November 2018. According to the Seattle Times the company was mired under heavy debts and hammered by the falling prices in Bitcoin. Bad timing for this Bitcoin pioneer. I left the information on Giga Watt in this book as they have been one of the largest players in Bitcoin. Taking place in the Bitcoin Capital of the World, at one point, David Carlson, co-founder of Giga Watt had the largest Bitcoin mine in the world. I don't know what will happen to Giga Watt in the long run but maybe it will be reincarnated by some means, possibly by an investment group or other entity.

Bitmain is a privately-owned company that specializes in the manufacturing and development of Bitcoin and cryptocurrency mining devices. Bitmain is located in China with offices all over the world. Bitmain has also been a growing Bitcoin mining operator and owner/operator of AntPool, Hashnest, and BTC.com. AntPool is one of the world's largest mining pools, where Bitcoin miners of the world join their computing power together, increasing the overall hashing power, increasing the odds of solving blocks with the Bitcoin reward being distributed evenly among all miners in the pool (share based on one's individual computing power). Hashnest is a cloud mining service similar to Giga Watt. BTC.com is a service providing software for Bitcoin and Bitcoin Cash

(BCH) wallets and software interface to mine BTC/BCH mining pools. Bitmain also develops artificial intelligence (AI) computer chips and other AI technology.

Bitmain has recently announced its first ever US-based Bitcoin mining operation. Approved by the US government, the state of Washington, and the southwest region of Washington state, the region of Walla Walla. Bitmain has also announced another 500-million-dollar Bitcoin mining operation to be constructed in Milam County, Texas. This operation in Texas alone will provide the area over 400 jobs.

Update: Bitmain now has a large Bitcoin mining operation in East Wenatchee right in the heart of the Bitcoin Capital of the World. They also announced the plans to build 17 other Bitcoin mining operations across the United States. Bitmain is a fast-growing billion-dollar company that is invested heavily in Bitcoin, Bitcoin and cryptocurrency mining, and blockchain data centers all over the world. Bitmain is near 51% but drawing close. Keep an eye on this situation.

Bitmain is probably the number one entity you need to keep an eye on as they are always 10 steps ahead of everyone else when it comes to Bitcoin, Bitcoin mining, and world establishment of blockchain technology and infrastructure. Keep your finger on the pulse of Bitcoin through Bitmains movements. If Bitmain ever goes public with the company, you better believe I will be investing in the Initial Public Offering(IPO).

Blockchain has got bankers of the world squirming and many industries interested in incorporating it into their systems. There are a multitude of industries, companies, and financial entities working on the development of blockchain technology. Blockchain is finding use in healthcare and life sciences, oil and gas, financial services, banking, supply chain management, government ledgers and smart contracts, security, and compliance, just to name a few.

Chapter Eight

Here are some up and coming blockchain systems you may want to monitor...

Amazon Web Services (AWS) is investing tons into blockchain services and partnerships. If Amazon (one of the wealthiest companies on earth) is investing in blockchain, then we should probably be paying attention. Check out the article "Amazon Partners On New Ethereum Marketplace For Enterprises" on Forbes.com.

There are many other big leaguers involved in the development of blockchain technology, including T-Mobile (JAZZ), Intel (Sawtooth-Hyperledger Project), Microsoft (Azure), PWC, Guidewire, Kaleido, Pokitdok, insurance company VSP (visionplans), Corda R3, Samsung Nexledger, Quorum, BlockApps, Deloitte, ShoCard, Luno, Coinbase, and many others.

The list is growing in this red-hot tech space. Other than Bitcoin, cryptocurrency, mining, and AI, blockchain is a must to monitor to keep your finger on the pulse.

Chapter Eight

CHAPTER NINE

UPGRADING A BITCOIN MINING OPERATION

As I've been writing this book, I've realized that my Spondoolies are great yet are becoming obsolete. I need to replace them with more power efficient and higher production Bitcoin miners. My Spondoolies run at 2400 watts each at 5 terahash (TH) mining capacity compared to newer Bitcoin miners like the Antminer S9 which runs at about 1350 watts with a 14 TH mining capacity. Terahash or TH/s is a measure of cryptocurrency or Bitcoin mining. One terahash is a performance of 1 trillion hashing operations a second.

In early 2018, I decided that my Spondoolies needed to go and a mining equipment upgrade was in order. The best Bitcoin miners available at the time were the Antminer S9s, mining at 14 TH/s each. They use half the power of my Spondoolies SP31s and mine at four times the mining performance which correlates to improved profit or earnings. I figured out my current power availability and decided on a new mining rig using 12 Antminer S9s running on 220 volts for a 14 TH/s mining workload each. This is going to increase my Bitcoin mining operation from 28 to 168 TH/s. This is six times more mining productivity.

The cost for this upgrade? Through the manufacture Bitmain the twelve Antminer S9s are $1,158 each, plus power supply at $115 each, for a total of $15,276 plus tariffs, shipping, customs, and other various fees. Basically, about $20,000. Twenty grand! ***These are the prices in the spring of 2018.***

This is still definitely way more affordable than ordering off eBay or some other retailer. The catch? Bitmain at the time only accepts Bitcoin Cash or Bitcoin for payment. Bitcoin cash which is cryptocurrency forked off the Bitcoin blockchain, sharing the pre-fork blockchain ledger but with its own blockchain post fork. Bitcoin cash is not Bitcoin it is an altcoin (alternative to Bitcoin) or cryptocurrency. Bitcoin is king and will always be in the world of blockchain.

As a Bitcoin miner, I hold tight to my Bitcoin. The last thing I want to do is spend it. I'm holding on to my Bitcoin for the long-term payout. I'm thinking about retirement in 2030, and my Bitcoin investments will help this happen. One thing for sure is I don't just have twenty grand floating in the couch cushions. I sat down with my pen, paper, and calculator app to figure it all out. The return on investment (ROI) for spending 2.2 Bitcoin on a mining rig upgrade was an obvious choice. The investment will increase my mining capacity by six times, according to Crypto Compare or Coinwarz.com, which are online Bitcoin mining calculators. These mining calculators figure out your mining profit based on your mining operations hash rate, the difficulty of mining at the time, the value of

Chapter Nine

Bitcoin at the time, minus your local power costs and mining pool fees.

I created an account on Bitmain's website and loaded up the shopping cart with 12 Antminer S9s at 14 TH each and 12 APW3 power supplies. I used my Ledger Nano S cryptocurrency cold storage wallet and executed the sending of 2.2 Bitcoin for payment. A little scary sending my Bitcoin to a company in China. A country on the other side of the planet! Within a couple minutes the transaction was completed. I received payment confirmation and verification that my order was being processed. Sure enough, the Bitcoins were gone from my wallet and the transaction recorded on the blockchain. OMG (Oh My Gosh)! "This is way too convenient," I said to myself. This is when the true reality of using cryptocurrency in commerce hit me. No middleman or bank to deal with! No pile of gold to haul to China. A super-fast transfer of money to a company across the planet! An incorruptible record of the transaction on the blockchain, and no mailing, shipping, or couriers of money.

It was like I pulled the money out of my wallet and personally handed it over to the seller, Bitmain in China. Wow! Super cool. This is so significant that I had to say to myself, "This is the future." When people try this out, they will be in disbelief how simple, fast, and efficient it is to use Bitcoin or other cryptocurrencies. This is the inevitable future, the digital age.

A few days later, I received an email and text confirmation from Bitmain that my order had shipped. They gave me a UPS tracking number and voila, items shipped! I waited in anticipation. A couple days later I received a call from UPS Customs Brokerage requesting my information and Social Security number to verify my identification and complete the international clearance process. This did have an additional cost of $400 that I was not planning on. It sort of freaked me out, but I verified the existence of UPS Customs Brokerage and it was legit. I paid the clearance fee in US dollars and two days later the UPS driver pulled up to our door.

What a glorious day! The packaging was not discrete. The words Antminer and Bitmain are on all sides of each box. I guess most non-miners have no clue what an Antminer even is, so it doesn't really matter. I mean, it's not like I was receiving a shipment of gold or something...or was I!?

What an exciting time for me. Next, I became a little worried as I knew I had to shut down my current Spondoolies mining operation and swap out all the mining gear. I fretted about how long my mining operation would be down and if the new Antminer S9s would work without a hitch, or if they'd be difficult to set up. I planned to do the big swap on my next day off work.

On the day of the big swap it was a little sad to shut down my good old Spondoolies miners, but exciting at the same time thinking about how the Antminer S9s would perform and how much more money I'd be making.

Overall getting the Antminers setup in my server rack was simple and streamlined. The custom S9 server-rack mounts I bought through Newegg made the install easy. The miners powered right up, and I searched my intranet for the individual IP addresses of the S9s. I was able to enter their programming window. I set up the mining pools, my receiving wallet address and boom! I was mining again.

Over the next week I observed the difference and sure enough the deposits of Bitcoin into my wallet were adding up much faster six times more productive and profitable than with my old gear. Definitely worth the investment. Now I can just sit back and relax while my twelve Antminer S9s hum along and do their job.

CHAPTER TEN

GRAYSCALE

I made $22,000 in 72 hours! In the spring of 2017. I figured out that there were new ways to invest in Bitcoin other than just buying or mining it. There are companies in the stock market, trust and mutual funds dabbling in Bitcoin and cryptocurrencies.

One option in particular caught my eye was Grayscale Bitcoin Trust Company, or Bitcoin Investment Trust, stock ticker GBTC. Grayscale caught my eye because number one I had no extra money to invest in Bitcoin or Bitcoin-related companies, but I did have a 401(k).

My 401(k) is through my work and the company managing it is Fidelity. Through Fidelity you can setup a special purchasing account called a brokerage link (if your employer allows this option).

The brokerage link allows you to go beyond the traditional funds offered in your employer plan by giving you access to thousands of mutual funds. In fact, over 11,000 options at the time. Some of the options are high risk and with higher fees. Through my brokerage link account, I searched out Bitcoin and, low and behold, one option popped up: Grayscale Investment Trust. I looked over my 401(k) funds and decided to exchange $18,000 in underperforming funds for shares in GBTC.

Over the next few days I would sign into my 401(k) account at work to see how the fund was performing. Now normally I'm not checking my 401(k) investments daily, but in the first day GBTC went up 28%. Let me repeat: 28%! For those who don't know this is an unrealistic return on investment (ROI) even for someone who is very passionate about anything Bitcoin.

So, 72 hours later, my $18,000 investment in Grayscale was now valued at a little over $40,000. At the time this was just too much for me to handle and I decided to cash out, leaving me with about a $22,000 profit in 3 days.

I've never made money this fast in my life. That's over $300 an hour for 72 hours straight. But…What a mistake to sell! Had I just held on like my instincts told me, I could have profited over $300,000 six months later.

In January of 2018, the Grayscale Bitcoin Investment Trust completed a 91-for-1 stock split. This lowered the price of one share from $1800 to about $19 dollars. Much more palatable to the average investor.

At the time of writing this book GBTC is at a value of four to five dollars a share, a steal of a deal if you believe in the future of Bitcoin. If Bitcoin increases to, let's say, $50,000 a coin in 2020, then GBTC would be about $71 dollars a share value for GBTC.

CHAPTER ELEVEN

CRYPTOCURRENCIES

From January 2017 to December 2017 Bitcoin appreciated from about $800 each to over $19,000 each. Anything Bitcoin related was blowing up. I bought shares in a penny stock company called Bitcoin Service, stock ticker BTSC. I made a $5000 profit on a $1500 investment. Even so, it can feel like the Bitcoin train has already left the station...or has it?

Fortunately, another growing area of investments is non-Bitcoin cryptocurrencies. Through cryptocurrency exchanges a person can buy "altcoins." Altcoin is used to describe any cryptocurrency that is not Bitcoin, though most cryptocurrencies or altcoins trade using Bitcoin as the store of value through cryptocurrency exchanges.

I did not get involved in these until it was too late to catch the initial rise in value, over 7000% for some. Some cryptocurrencies grew more rapidly than Bitcoin and were turning working class people into millionaires.

Chapter Eleven

Well, I am an investor in cryptocurrencies now. There are some good crypto exchanges out there. I use the Bittrex exchange and have invested Bitcoin that I earned from mining. Some of the cryptocurrencies I've invested in are Bitcoin Cash, Bitcoin Gold, Ripple, Verge, Geocoin, and some others.

Most of all I wanted to get involved with the altcoins supporting the cannabis industry financial infrastructure. I'm curious to see what happens value-wise to cannabis as countries and states legalize marijuana. The price of these cryptocurrencies may go through the roof. This is my play, but it's all high risk in the land of cryptocurrencies, so tread forth carefully. I am in no way a financial advisor and am only sharing my ideas and thoughts on the matter. I'm just a regular working-class dude having some fun taking risks with my own money.

Here's a list of just some of the Altcoins or Cryptocurrencies:

Bitcoin (BTC)
Vechain (VET)
Digibyte (DGB)
Ethereum (ETH)
Binance Coin (BNB)
Bitshares (BTS)
XRP (XRP)
Tezos (XTZ)
Potcoin (POT)
Bitcoin Cash (BCH)
Zcash (ZEC)
Maker (MKR)
EOS (EOS)
OmiseGo (OMG)
Aeternity (AE)
Stellar (XLM)
Dogecoin (DOGE)

Chapter Eleven

Verge (XVG)
Litecoin (LTC)
Lisk (LSK)
Steem (STEEM)
Tether (USDT)
Bytecoin (BCN)
Siacoin (SC)
Cardano (ADA)
Ontology (ONT)
Augur (REP)
Monero (XMR)
0x (ZRX)
Bytom (BTM)
IOTA (MIOTA)
Qtum (QTM)
BitcoinDiamond (BCD)
Dash (DASH)
Nano (NANO)
Golem (GNT)
Tron (TRX)
Bitcoin Gold (BTG)
Reddcoin (RDD)
NEO (NEO)
Decred (DCR)
Ark (ARK)
Ethereum Classic (ETC)
ICON (ICX)
Bitcoin Private (BTCP)
NEM (XEM)
Zilliga (ZIL)
Geocoin (GEO)

There are so many more. If you're interested in seeing how many other cryptocurrencies options there are a good reference is to check out the Markets tab on the Bittrex exchange (www.bittrex.com). Each altcoin has its own take on security, blockchain, smart contracts, cloud storage, energy, privacy, anonymity, financial transactions, with industry-specific branding and aim toward a smarter economy.

I'm going to end here on cryptocurrencies. As far as blockchain and altcoins go, the king will always be Bitcoin. In my vision of the future, I see Bitcoin as gold and cryptocurrencies as each country's, states, cities, industrys, companys, or whatever's unique way of handling money. Bitcoin is the store of value between all cryptocurrencies and at only 21 million or less total Bitcoins the value of one Bitcoin can exponentially rise to untold wealth. Just give it time.

Remember my Bitcoin meme on the "coin verse" from the movie *The Lord of the Rings*, with my own little twist:

One coin to rule them all
One coin to find them
One coin to bring them all
And in the darkness bind them.

— — — — — — —

CHAPTER TWELVE

BLOCKCHAIN. WHAT IS IT?

First off, I would like to say that blockchain technology is far too complex and its current worldwide development is much to vast to fully capture its essence in just one chapter. I will keep this chapter short and sweet with just the basics of the Bitcoin blockchain. After reading this book I recommend reading a book solely dedicated to blockchain technology as it is the future of the digital frontier, just like Bitcoin. I have read and recommend the book "Blockchain for dummies" by Tiana Laurence. Just know she is a co-founder/stakeholder in Factom a blockchain company. She does push Factom a bit throughout the book but does remain on topic with the industry.

The Bitcoin blockchain is a publicly distributed ledger recording all Bitcoin transactions since its inception in 2009. It is decentralized, meaning the power is in the hands of the individual users and not on one central authority. Because of the

Chapter Twelve

decentralized essence of blockchain the possible technological advances are unprecedented.

How is this accomplished? Well, it is through Bitcoin mining. Imagine that there are one million Bitcoin mining operations on earth currently. That's at least one million computers that have the entire Bitcoin blockchain (or ledger) stored on their hard drives or servers. These one million miners have a ledger of all past, present, and potential future transactions recorded and stored on the Bitcoin blockchain, which is again stored on over one million miners' computers, servers, or hard drives.

Each transaction made on the blockchain is verified by the many miners computing power and blockchain ledgers to secure the transactions validity and record it. It takes at least six confirmations to secure or validate then record a transaction on the Bitcoin blockchain. For this reason, Bitcoin cannot be counterfeited, stolen, or destroyed. The only way to lose it completely at this point is if the hardware is lost, damaged, or gone and you lost or misplace your private key, then kiss it good bye.

A dollar bill or quarter can be counterfeited simply by remaking their physical attributes as best possible. A Bitcoin is digital and consists of a 512 bit chain code, including 256 for a private key and 256 for a public key. Bitcoin cannot transact without the "secret" or private key code. As long as you have your private keys you control your Bitcoin. When you buy something using Bitcoin, you enter your private key in to a "send transaction" from your digital Bitcoin wallet.

The Bitcoin blockchain or network will verify: 1) the Bitcoin in connection with the private key have not been spent already, and 2) the transaction will be verified by at least six different Bitcoin mining nodes. Thus confirmed, your Bitcoin will transfer to the other party.

This transaction cannot be reversed. The Bitcoin you sent belongs to a new address with newly assigned private keys. A record of your transaction will be recorded into the Bitcoin blockchain and this record is stored on every single Bitcoin miners' servers or hard drives. Literally millions of receipts.

I can see the U.S. Social Security system benefiting from switching to a blockchain type ledger of identity verification, recording, and security. And holy smokes can we do away with the pre-historic and high risk paper SSI cards and switch to a hard card with computer chip and password security.

Again this is just a little snippet into blockchain. If you want to understand it better then research the topic. There is a plethora of information available. Amazon.com has many eBooks, paper, hardback, or audio books available on blockchain and have a reliable reviews and rating system. On Amazon website go to Kindle eBooks and in the search bar type in blockchain and search. Featured books and reviews will be presented.

Ethereum Mining Rig running 8 Video Cards.

The LED glow inside a Bitcoin mining server. Servertec PDUs mounted on sides.

CHAPTER THIRTEEN

BITCOIN IN USE

The other day I was tempted to spend some of my Bitcoin on a fire-engine red Dodge Viper RT10 convertible. Then on a Humvee. I didn't pull the trigger though, because some day I know that same amount of Bitcoin will buy me 10 Vipers or 10 Humvees. This near miss almost happened through Craigslist. Luckily my wife talked some sense into me. The Viper was for sale through a dealer in Seattle that accepts cryptocurrency for payment, and the Humvee was through a private party willing to take cryptocurrency as well.

All that is needed to complete the transaction is your Bitcoin wallet either through an app, a laptop, tablet, paper wallet (a paper print or of the public key and private key together with a barcode also considered a type of cold storage), and that brings us to my favorite method, which is a cold storage device, like Ledger Nano S, Blue, or Trezor. From your Bitcoin wallet you go to Send coins or Send tab, enter the receiving address in the

Chapter Thirteen

Pay To: area, which is the seller's Bitcoin wallet (Car dealer or private party in this case), then finally enter the BTC amount in the ***Amount*** area and hit ***Send*** at the bottom. In moments the transaction is verified and recorded into the blockchain. Then the amount of Bitcoin entered transfers from your wallet to the seller's. Voila! Now you're the proud new owner of a fire-engine red Dodge Viper.

The above Viper deal almost happened, but if I had pulled the trigger and drove home with a convertible, my wife would've probably cut off my balls and hung them from the rearview mirror. (My proof reader did not like this joke...too violent).

Come on! I'm just kidding here. Just thought some humor was due. She would never hang'em from the mirror like that!

...Okay, seriously now.

There are other methods to pay for something using Bitcoin. For example, Visa offers debit cards, and one is through a company called Bitpay. Bitpay takes care of "Bitcoin to cash" exchanges no different than your regular debit card. It's no different from moving money from your traditional bank debit card to the seller's account. The advantage using Bitcoin is the speed, convenience, and record of sale on the indestructible Bitcoin blockchain.

Bitcoin use is growing exponentially. On August 31, 2018, Bitcoin transactions reached a higher value then PayPal. Can you say that again?

Bitcoin transaction value exceeds PayPal!

It's crazy to me, but most people I mention Bitcoin to still blow it off as a joke. Most people remain blind to Bitcoin, cryptocurrency, and what is happening to the world of finance around them.

There are many businesses that accept Bitcoin for payment or

Chapter Thirteen

offer Bitcoin or cryptocurrency as optional payment methods. Here is a list of companies that are Bitcoin friendly at the time of writing this book. I'm not going into detail on the company and their use or plans with Bitcoin. I recommend to Google them individually if you're curious. There are resources available, one is the article ***How to Use Bitcoin for Purchases*** at thestreet.com.

Here it goes! Bitcoin in use at the time of writing this book.
This list is increasing over time:

Craigslist
Visa Bitpay
Auto Dealers
Private Party Sales
Overstock.com
Microsoft
Expedia
Newegg
Shopify
DishNet
Playboy
KFC Canada
Subway
Virgin Galactic
Wikipedia
93 separate Etsy dealers
Whole Foods
Intuit
Re-Max London
Bitcoin ATMs (worldwide)

Bitcoin ATM's are also popping up all over the world. I sometimes wonder how lucrative being a Bitcoin ATM vendor is? This might be a good business model to look in to. The state of Ohio is the first state to allow taxes to be paid in Bitcoin. It's very exciting to watch the Bitcoin empire develop and become part of the economy. I am looking forward to seeing name brands like Samsung, Apple, Sony, and Panasonic come out with cold storage Bitcoin/cryptocurrency wallets. You hear that Samsung! We are ready and waiting for your high-quality Bitcoin wallet product. Bring it on!

― ― ― ― ― ―

CHAPTER FOURTEEN

THE DIGITAL AGE

Go on any major news station's stock market analysis, financial, or economic reports and you'll see that Bitcoin is here to stay. Bitcoin is slashed with US dollar (USD/BTC) in currency reports. Instead of slashing USD with some other big league world currency or even with gold... it is slashed with Bitcoin (BTC). I mean, come on! Even if you're in doubt, you've got to be able to see the significance of this. Well, I do, and that's why I'm investing in the Bitcoin economy and blockchain technology. Digital money is already a fact of life. Think about every payment and/or purchase you make. It's done with the push of a touch screen, mouse click, debit swipe, or chip reader. Cash and coins are becoming obsolete. Digital currency is the now and the future. So let's talk about what the digital age holds for us.

As the world economy develops, fewer and fewer Third

Chapter Fourteen

World countries are without power, cellular, and Internet. More and more people become customers and consumers within the world's currency systems.

First off lets discuss what a store of value is. A store of value is anything with value that can be stored, held, saved and is retrievable at a later time. Some examples of a store of value are real estate, cattle, money and precious metals or gems.

Gold has long been many nations primary store of value in the history of man back to 600 BC. With most money exchanges taking place on the Internet, how can gold remain the world's store of value as all currency transactions eventually become digital? The answer is, it can't. Gold cannot remain the world's store of value in the digital age.

Bitcoin is poised to replace gold, and cryptocurrencies to replace the unique currency for each country. Each nation could have its own blockchain-backed cryptocurrency and behind it Bitcoin for international trading, purchasing, or selling. Anybody or any entity can make their own cryptocurrency, give it a name, offer it as coin or token, and use the blockchain accounting ledger to record all transactions or business operations. Not that a new cryptocurrency will automatically have value, but if you look at the history of initial coin offerings (ICOs, similar to IPO or initial public offering of a stock company but in cryptocurrency) then you'll see that people invest massive amounts of money into them.

Imagine a future when all the governments of our world replace their fiat currencies with a digital currency and blockchain technology. How about the USA? The new currency can be named anything, including a name like US Dollar. Or something new and catchy like Americoin, USAcoin, or FreedomCoin. In fact, each state can have its own cryptocurrency or blockchain. Calicoin, NYcoin, or Florideum.

Go even deeper and each county or city can have their own digital currency and blockchain. Right down to corporations,

Chapter Fourteen

businesses, and individuals. Google Coin, Dutchbrocoin, and Yourcoin. The ability to use digital currency can transfer from the most basic of transactions to a universal scale, even planet to planet. All digital currencies with the security and accountability of the blockchain and all communicating and exchanging between or among each other using one universal store of value: Bitcoin.

Bitcoin will be the store of value that each unique digital currency can trade within and with ease. All transactions recorded in the blockchain. Like we all need air to breath, cryptocurrencies need a way to trade between each other, for example from fictional Americoin to Chinacoin. This is where Bitcoin comes in. Bitcoin is the air that cryptocurrencies breath. Bitcoin comes in and out of sending and receiving transactions to trade value through the use of digital currency exchanges. Or without the middleman peer to peer, wallet to wallet. It doesn't matter how many different cryptocurrencies there are. Each cryptocurrency can trade value between each other using Bitcoin as the value transfer or store of value. Every person, nation, government, continent, planet...earthcoin, galaxy... Marscoin, and universe can exchange value between one another using their unique cryptocurrencies using Bitcoin as the store of value.

Here's an example. I just exchanged Potcoin for Geocoin using the Bittrex exchange. The exchange takes my Potcoin out of my wallet and transfers it to equal value in Bitcoin, then takes that value in Bitcoin and purchases that value in Geocoin, and then deposits it in my Geocoin wallet. Voila! I just exchanged my Potcoin from my Potcoin wallet to equal value of Geocoin in my Geocoin wallet using Bitcoin as a store of value and the Bittrex exchange as the facilitator. It's that easy, super-fast, secure, and a record of the transaction is stored on the blockchain.

For comparison, just try trading US dollars (USD) for

Chapter Fourteen

Mongolian tugriks (MNT)(or any other nation's currency for that matter). It won't be so simply done as the Potcoin to Geocoin example above. You can try using an online exchange like Travelex, which limits you to about 50 different currencies, not including tugriks.

With Travelex you can order other countries currencies online and have them delivered by mail to your front door. Wow! How many times have we been told not to send cash in the mail? This is a very low-tech, unsophisticated, and insecure means to obtain another nation's currency in preparation for travel to that country. There are fees for using this process, of course. You could also physically drive and walk to your local bank and try to obtain the foreign currency you need and pay the fees. But I bet your local bank will not have tugriks on hand and will have to order the value you need through (you guessed it!)the mail. You might be able to exchange your money at the airport or use a foreign ATM to convert your USD to another currency with a fee or use a credit card but, remember, you're going to Mongolia and good luck finding an ATM that will give you tugriks for dollars or hope that the place you want to spend money will accept your credit card.

This whole process is made super simple using Bitcoin and the blockchain accounting ledger. In the possible future, the US will have its own cryptocurrency, let's call it Americoin, and Mongolia will have its own too, let's call it Mongolicoin. In preparation for your travel to Mongolia, all you have to do is download a Mongolicoin wallet to your smart phone, Ledger Nano S, Trezor, or laptop computer. Then use an online exchange like Bittrex, Bittfinex, or Binance to trade Americoin from your Americoin wallet to Bitcoin, then to Mongolicoin into your Mongolicoin wallet. Now you can use your Mongolicoin in Mongolia. This process only takes minutes and can take place anywhere there is Internet access. Presto!

As every year passes technology advances quicker. This is

Chapter Fourteen

the digital age. We are approaching a time where paper money, checks, coins, and even plastic cards will be obsolete. Why would we hang on to these low-tech financial tools when a tiny computer chip (and I mean tiny) can be implanted under your skin and contain hundreds of different digital currencies, currency wallets, driver's license, passports, work identification, credentials, medical history, allergies, club cards, and all minus the cards? The amount of digital information is nearly endless and can be uploaded, downloaded, or deleted as you need.

With your new digital ID, you can just walk into an airport and the door scanners will instantly identify you, your tickets, and then you're ready to check in your bags without the hassle of passports and gate checks. With your digital ID, you will not have to flash a single card as you walk in. The door scanner will instantly identify you, verify your membership is current, and check you in as "Shopping" or "Travelling" status. The possibilities are endless. For example, you can be identified at the door of your home, your car, work, the gym, etc. The digital ID will free you of having to carry around a clunky keychain full of keys and fobs. OMG! No more wallet. No more keys on key chains. No more waiting in line for an identity check in and check out. All this information is right there at all times, weightless, and ready to be scanned. You won't have to worry about forgetting your wallet, your keys, or your money. No more worrying about my wife leaving her purse or credit cards pocketed on her smart phone somewhere.

The technology of going digital is endless. Imagine as you walk out of your home you verbalize a word like leaving, and your home identifies who you are by your voice and digital ID chip. It then automatically shuts the door, locks the deadbolt, and sets the alarm. Next, as you approach your car you say, "open," your identity is confirmed, the car unlocks itself, starts, and all your personal settings are established. As you enter the car you hear, "What is your destination today?" "The Bitcoin

Chapter Fourteen

farm" you state, and instantly the GPS maps out the quickest route, avoiding all construction, traffic congestion, and accidents. As you're driving to your Bitcoin mining operation, you realize that you forgot to order that new fitness watch your spouse wanted for their birthday coming up. Driving down the road you verbalize, "Alexa," and proceed to complete your order on Amazon online. All instantaneous because your car knows who you are based on your voice and implanted digital information microchip. Your Bitcoin wallet is setup to pay and boom! The transaction, payment, and shipping information is all complete. All while driving down the road.

I can go on and on with ideas for the future of having a digital ID, digital wallet, and digital information of everything else in your purse or wallet. My dog has an information microchip implant. I'll let your mind run wild now.

There are books on the matter like, "Innovative Automatic Identification and Location-Based Services, from bar codes to chip implants," by Katrina and M.G. Michael. For this to become possible the Internet must be available everywhere you go. Eventually the entire earth, space stations, and moon will be 100% covered in Wi-Fi. Life is going to get easier and easier, and the ability to pay for things more simple and secure. If you don't want an implant then there will be other less secure means of identification like a jewelry, watches, or other technological devices with an I.D. microchip installed.

Most people around me seem oblivious, turning their heads to Bitcoin and the digital age. People may need a slap to the face or a cattle prod to the ass to capture their attention. I mean, with all the evidence around them, they continue to be in disbelief that Bitcoin and cryptocurrencies are real. The Bitcoin technological breakthrough is obvious and occurring right now right before our eyes.

Chapter Fourteen

Do you want to be a loser or a winner in the game?
Are you even going to play?

$$$$$$$

Chapter Fourteen

Olympia Washington capital building on Veterans Day...a beautiful day to capture the book's cover image.

Aerial view of the Wenatchee/East Wenatchee valley.
Center of the Bitcoin Capital of the World.

CHAPTER FIFTEEN

HOW TO ACHIEVE WEALTH, HEALTH, AND WELLNESS

As a health and wellness coach, power lifter, competitive bodybuilder, hospital therapist, and certified fitness trainer, this chapter title is my twist on the classic health and wellness.

"What the hell does this have to do with Bitcoin mining?" You might ask yourself. Well, I hate to break it to you, but life's not all about Bitcoin. Now, don't get me wrong, I'm very passionate about Bitcoin, Bitcoin mining, cryptocurrency, and the future of blockchain technology, but success isn't so one-sided.

If you are reading this book, then I know you care about your financial future and are interested in Bitcoin and how it may become part of your investment portfolio. I have lived through some great investment experiences, including startup

Chapter Fifteen

businesses, stock market, real estate, social media, Roth, 401(k), cryptocurrency trading, and Bitcoin mining. Here I want to share my ideas on achieving a great finances as well as a healthy life. Because, without health, you have nothing.

I have learned that health cannot be achieved if you are in a poor financial situation, and vice versa. Ultimate wealth will not bring you happiness without a healthy body and mind. So, the way I look at it, we must strive to achieve our best possible state of health and wealthness.

••••••••••••••••••••••••

Health and wealthness, wealth and healthness, health, wealth, and wellness, however you want to state it...I define as: *a state of harmony in life, with the perfect balance of education, work, debt, exercise, investments, assets, love, nutrition, spirituality, more hard work, rest, and (you guessed it) Bitcoin!*

••••••••••••••••••••••••

Let's start out talking about wealth and how to hold onto yours.

Wealth: Pay Yourself First

Education is first, but after that, what's next? If you are able to work at a job you are passionate about, then start investing in yourself financially. PAY YOURSELF FIRST. What do I mean by pay yourself first? It's a confusing quote you read about repeatedly when dealing with your money, investments, and especially retirement accounts. The main idea behind this quote is to put a percentage of your paycheck into a pre-tax 401(k) or Roth401(k), or other retirement vehicle. Whether you are getting paid by an employer or self-employed, the

Chapter Fifteen

government offers incentives to divert some of your money into retirement savings.

Taking advantage of pre-tax investments is an absolute must. For one, it decreases your income tax burden. Here's an example: let's say you make $100,000 a year. You must pay taxes on $100,000. If you invest 20% of that $100,000 into a 401(k), then you have $20,000 saved in your 401(k) and only pay taxes on $80,000. So not only do you pay less taxes ($80k-vs-$100k), you also have twenty frickin grand in the bank that will sit there gaining interest, leading to compounding interest into infinity.

Another means of pre-tax savings investments is through an HSA (Health Savings Account). This works the same as a 401(k) in that it takes a percentage of your earnings pre-tax and puts it into a savings account that can be used for healthcare expenses. This investment again decreases your tax burden. Let's look at the previous example for the 401(k). First you invested 20% of your $100,000 income, which is $20,000 in 401(k). Now you also contribute 5% to your HSA, which is $5,000. This leaves you with a $75,000 tax burden. Now you have $20,000 in your 401(k) and $5,000 in your HSA and pay taxes on only $75,000 instead of $100,000.

The financial leverage of these investment opportunities over time is incredible.

If you take advantage of these pay-yourself-first pre-tax investments over the course of 10 years, the end result is very fruitful, because now you can add the passive income of compounding interest. For this example below, we will use a modest interest of 5% annual growth over the course of 10 years, putting 20% of your $100,000 paycheck into your 401(k), and 5% into your HSA.

Chapter Fifteen

The results are as follows:

Income	$1,000,000	$1,000,000
	Contributing	NOT Contributing
Pre-Tax 401(k)	$200,000	0
Pre-Tax HSA	$50,000	0
Taxable Income	$750,000	$1,000,000
Tax bracket	15% = $112,500	25% = $250,000
Employer Contribution to 401(k)	$40,000	0
10 years interest earned	$423,719	0
Actual overall 10-year income, including take home pay, 401(k), HSA, employer contributions and compound interest.	After taxes… $637,500 income $200,000 401(k) $50,000 HSA $40,000 employer cont. $423,719 interest	After taxes… $750,000 income 0 0 0 0
10-year accrual/Total	$1,351,219	$750,000
PAY!	YOURSELF!	FIRST!

Let's say it all together, **"Pay Yourself First!"**
That's a difference of $601,219 in a 10 year period.

It is absolute stupidity to not put money in the tax deferred opportunities at your discretion in order to save, invest in your future, and decrease your overall tax burden annually. Knowing how powerful an income tool paying yourself first is, then it's obvious every income earner should invest the maximum yearly allowable amount into a 401(k), IRA, Roth, and HSA.

Health

The pay-yourself-first rule not only applies to investing in your financial future but also your body and mind. Investing now in your physical and mental assets pays dividends later. Just like your financial portfolio, the more you invest in your body and mind the more valuable your physical assets (your brain, heart, lungs, etc.) will be in the future.

For example, a human body that is NOT invested in with

exercise, eating right, and spiritual healing will have a very low value in the future due to the negative effects of being sedentary, eating poorly, and losing spiritual focus. A person who invests exercise, prayer or meditation, and eats a restrictive or lean diet will have the highest value—physical existence in the future. The lower the amount you invest in your body, the higher the negative health disparity, such as diseases and disabilities in later years. The more you invest in exercise, weight training, and other physical activity, the stronger, longer, and better performance will benefit you in old age.

What do you invest into your body and mind to maximize your health and wellness? You invest time in exercise daily, eating lean protein and nutritious fruits and vegetables, as well as time spent in relaxation, meditation, prayer, and spirituality.

The more you invest in yourself (pay yourself first), the better your health, wealth, and wellness will be. Like I tell my clients, "The more you pay yourself first, the happier you will be." This is because wealth, good health, and wellness lead to an improved quality of life.

Real Estate

As I described earlier, I have a decent amount of experience in residential and commercial real estate investments. I don't want to spend very much time talking about real estate investing because there are so many good books and resources out there to guide you if you choose to invest in real estate, which I highly recommend. I'll summarize the basic highlights of real estate investing as I see it.

Commercial real estate is difficult to finance when compared to residential, but is very rewarding, due to the fact that you can write off most expense involved. You also can usually command higher rent income.

Residential real estate is a great way to own your home and

at the same time improve it to increase its value. The longer you own your home the more equity you will have due to slowly paying the loan down through mortgage payments plus the added value of real estate appreciation. Another cool thing to know about residential real estate is that, if you lived in your home at least two of the last five years then you pay NO taxes on up to $250,000 of the profit, or $500,000 if married filing jointly.

The long term and very valuable real estate investment is rentals. Whether you buy new home and rent out your old home, or rent out your current home, or invest in commercial real estate, with rentals you can achieve great wealth letting others pay off your mortgage for you. If you stick it out for the full term of the mortgage (typically twenty years for commercial or thirty years for residential), then you will have that much appreciation in value of the property, with nearly 100% equity because renters paid the mortgage for you.

Over thirty years a property you may have originally purchased for $150,000 could be worth $500,000 for your future retirement. If, over time, you acquire 10 rentals and manage them to the end of their term, that is $5,000,000. Read: five million dollars for your retirement. You could sell them for a great retirement or keep managing the 10 properties and earn passive income for the rest of your life. With that average rent in the US being $1,231 a month in 2018. Based on the current rent, that is $12,310 a month passive income. Imagine the rent 20 or 30 years from now, when your rentals are paid off. The monthly income would be much, much more.

My advice on real estate investments is to go long. It's more work but much more lucrative in the end. Short term real estate investments are risky and you can end up losing your shirt. Believe me, I've seen it happen.

Here are some books on real estate investments that provided me with benefit: Trump: "The Art of the Deal," "Why We

Chapter Fifteen

Want You To Be Rich," by Donald Trump and Robert Kyosaki, "Rich Dad Poor Dad" + "The Cashflow Quadrant" by Robert Kyosaki, and "The Millionaire Next Door" by Thomas J. Stanley and William D. Danko.

Buying Bitcoin and Altcoins

Of course, I believe that investing in Bitcoin and the blockchain technology as it unfolds is potentially the biggest opportunity in our lifetime to make the wealth part in health and wealthness. There are many different ways to invest in Bitcoin, blockchain, and cryptocurrencies.

You can straight up buy Bitcoin and cryptocurrencies and store them in a cold storage wallet. I am a buy-and-hold type on all Bitcoin investments. You can also invest in Grayscale Bitcoin Trust Fund, as I've done. One of the most popular and secure ways to buy Bitcoin is through Coinbase.

Another interesting way to invest in Bitcoin and cryptocurrencies (cryptos for short) is by day trading. (Erroneously named, as you can actually trade 24 hours a day, 7 days a week.) Just like the stock market, cryptos and Bitcoin can be bought and sold to capture profits on the ups and downs in pricing.

Of course, my favorite investment in Bitcoin is Bitcoin mining itself. I'm glad I started mining early and will continue to mine, upgrade, and grow my mining operation to meet the demands of exponentially growing mining difficulty over time. As this is the design of the Bitcoin coin mining difficulty algorithm. The mining algorithm is designed for it to make financial sense now and in the future when the value of Bitcoin is much higher. Over time you get less Bitcoin shares mining but also over time the value of Bitcoin goes up thus balancing the situation out. I plan to continue mining Bitcoin the rest of my life and into retirement in the year 2030 (my target retirement date may be earlier if Bitcoin explodes like Mt. Saint Helens). Bitcoin mining in retirement? I talk about this subject coming up in the next chapter of this book...

Get Ready! Its Coming!

Penny Stocks

Another great way to invest in possible long-term wealth is to build a penny stock portfolio. I like to throw my spare change at this, about 3.5% of my investment money. I use E-Trade to do my trading and to hold my penny stock assets. I like to invest in small Canadian and US oil companies like Blackbird Energy and Oil (BKBEF). I'm always watching for a good startup in the cannabis industry, as recreational marijuana is now legal in Canada and is making its way to legal status state by state in the US.

Just imagine how much money you could make if you invest in a small penny stock company that eventually becomes the next Phillip Morris or British America of the cannabis industry. The crypto coins of the cannabis industry definitely peak my interest, digital currencies like Potcoin (P) or Hempcoin (THC).

As the digital age is upon us and cannabis becomes as common as Marlboro Reds, there will need to be a digital asset for use in commerce. These early cryptos are working on the infrastructure, design, algorithms, blockchains, and protocols. When the time comes, they will be poised to take over the job of paper cash and metal coins for the cannabis industry.

When it comes to penny stocks it's fun to look for the right companies to invest in. You can invest in companies that interest you for whatever reason. Some other areas I'm watching for penny stock companies are in 3D printing, drone technology, nutritional supplements, computers, genetics, pharmaceuticals,

Chapter Fifteen

biotech, smart lighting, the Internet of Things (IOT) startups, new battery technology, fusion development, and young social media applications.

Investing in penny stocks is considered high risk and should only be invested in with money you *can afford to lose*. If the company goes broke, which they might, then you'll lose every penny invested. But whoa! if the company makes it big time, and you invested in the early stages, then you will make it big time too.

There are many different reputable platforms to setup your account and start building your long-term, buy-and-hold penny stock portfolio. Some well-known companies are E-Trade, Ameritrade, Acorns, Fidelity, Scottrade, and Robinhood. I have had great results using E-Trade and Fidelity.

One thought to always keep in mind when investing in penny stocks is: *the early bird gets the worm*. When it comes to penny stocks…well any investment, don't invest money you can't afford to lose! Penny stocks are high risk so know that going in.

Business

Having a business is another interesting wealth appreciation vehicle. I'm not a business man per se but I have experience with starting, owning, and selling a couple coffee shops. If you want to start up a business, I recommend you read as much as you can on the subject and interview as many business owners as you can before taking the plunge. Books that I have read and benefited me are: "Think and Grow Rich" by Napolean Hill, "How To Win Friends and Influence People" by Dale Carnegie, and "Principles: Life and Work" by Ray Dalio. I would like to share a little about when I learned about owning a business.

Starting up, managing, and owning a small business takes

money, time, and more time. The benefits of owning a business are way cool though. For starters, like commercial real estate, most expenses that go toward the business, its assets, equipment, vehicles, computers, travel expenses, etc. are tax write-offs.

The number one benefit of owning a business is the power and leverage gained by having increased cash flow. Positive or negative, banks love to see cash flow. The more money passes through your fingers, the easier it is to get loans on anything, from vehicles to equipment to other businesses and real estate.

I definitely recommend having a business on the side to increase cash flow, write off and depreciate applicable real estate, equipment, vehicles, and expenses.

Social Media/E-commerce

I just have to throw this one out there. The digital age is upon us and the Internet is a cornucopia of opportunities to leave your mark and make some money. I am going to focus on digital media in particular here.

Now, the digital media I'm talking about is the real stuff made by anybody who does the work, e.g. 4K videos on topics ranging from *gaming* to *how-to* to *travel* to *adventure* to *make-up*. The list of video types consumers will devour is infinite. Use your imagination! If you really want to add value to a video, add aerial video shots. Get your drone out or hire an FAA UAV (Unmanned Aircraft Vehicle) certified pilot to take some for you. Making high-quality videos is a great way to make extra money or cash flow, even as a primary source of income through ad revenue, Internet marketing, and social leveraging. A few places you can make money are YouTube, Twitch, Instagram, Facebook, Twitter, Tumbler, and of course your own personal or business website.

Another great way to add wealth with digital media is photography. Film is obsolete and digital cameras are becoming

Chapter Fifteen

so high tech that almost anyone can produce professional-grade photographs with a high-grade camera. I use the Nikon D500, a solid camera. Aerial photography is an absolute shiner and can add much value if you do the work. Just a few of the ways you can make money with digital photography is to put them on stock photo websites like Shutterstock, Adobe Stock, Snappa, Pexils, and your own website, of course.

Everyone has a story or a book inside them and can write it down, have it edited, then made into a digital media product placed on the Internet to sell as an e-book. Nowadays, it has become much easier to also have your book available in paperback or hard cover copy. You just have to do the work. Sit down and put your story on paper.

I found time to write this book by waking up at 3a.m. and writing until 5 a.m. every day. Then I got ready and went to my day job. At the time of writing this book I don't know if this book is hot or not, but at the minimum, if I sell one copy to a non-friend or family member, then I succeeded. And if you're reading this book, then it looks like I sold one. Score!

I made the time to write this book. Two hours a day writing and re-writing over the course of eight months doesn't seem like much, but when you add that up into an eight-hour work day then whoa! The reality is that I worked 60 straight days 8 hours a day on writing this book. "The power of two hours a day," I like to say. Sit down, write your book and put it out there for sale. Then write more books and put them out there. This could end up being the biggest wealth investment of your life. Well, except for Bitcoin of course!

I'm going to wrap up digital media on that note. Aside from your day job and Bitcoin mining from home, you can greatly add to your wealth by creating videos, aerial media, photography, or e-books, which you own forever and can add sales, royalties, and notoriety to your wealth portfolio.

Chapter Fifteen

The Body...your body: Low Risk

Okay now let's get down to the nitty-gritty. The most important component of achieving maximal health and wealthness is (you guessed it) your health. One sure thing is that each of us can bet on is death. Death is inevitable. Death is coming, but it's coming sooner or later, depending on the choices we make. The time in between birth and death is called life. The best way to measure life is not by time alone, but by quality of life over time, or QOL/Time. Most people focus on the length of life and not so much the quality. The quality of the life we live is far more important than the time we live it. Quality of life depends again on the choices we make as well as how we feed our bodies, the physical activity we engage in, and the stress we endure. We all want to live forever until our quality of life becomes poor. So, each one of us in our own puny existence should strive or take whatever means necessary to make sure we live the best and highest quality of life possible. What is possible depends on your actions.

Only some aspects of life are out of our control. Like our genetics, birth defects, mental illness, or handicaps, but what we choose to do with our given situation determines the quality life, regardless of our genetic lottery. We mustn't focus on things out of our control, but on the things we can control. We can control the choices we make, our goals, dreams, the actions we take, and how we choose to feel. Regardless our situation, we can choose to feel negative or positive about it. It just depends on how we choose to feel and where we put our focus. It's like I tell my kids, "Where focus goes, energy flows."

We control our actions toward achieving those goals. We control how we choose to feel during the highs and lows along our journey.

Chapter Fifteen

Meditation is a popular activity to re-center one's self. Meditation is a repeated process of training your mind to focus and direct your thoughts toward centeredness and balance. Some of the benefits of meditation are to increase awareness of one's self and one's surroundings. It can help reduce anxiety, increase emotional health, enhance self-awareness, improve attention, improve memory and quality of sleep, better our behavior and character, and help control or conquer addictions. Meditation can also provide other physical benefits of reduced pain or improved pain control and decreased blood pressure. Find peace!

Prayer is likely the most common activity used by most cultures of the world. Pray and pray often; it can provide a person with peace of mind and forgiveness. Prayer can also help achieve physical, emotional, mental, and spiritual healing. Prayer can help a person feel a sense of belonging, a sense of higher power, and a sense of purpose. Prayer helps people make the right decisions and turn away from wrong-doing or evil. Prayer reminds us how to behave and helps us know when to turn the other cheek, to forgive and forget as appropriate. Prayer can help you achieve a sense of great appreciation and grace. It can also help you find your center and establish balance of the body, mind, and soul.

Now that you're on the road to maximizing your health and wealthness, keep a vision of the *future you* in your mind for motivation. Imagine your paycheck being deposited for your work, your 401(k) building up, a building HSA and IRA, a stock portfolio growing with penny stocks, your side business and a couple rentals helping you increase cash flow and tax deductions. And, of course, your Bitcoin mining operation humming away twenty-four hours a day in your garage, increasing the value of your Bitcoin wallet. Your body is lean, toned, and strong. You're sleeping well and feeling great. You are at peace with the world around you and are in total control of yourself and your actions. You're eating is restrictive and necessary for the amount of activity you are engaging in and cravings for empty calorie foods and overeating are gone. All of your unhealthy habits are replaced with healthy habits and this is the new normal for you.

The vision of the future you is no myth, no joke. It is an accomplishment you will earn by taking control of your eating, exercise, recreation, socialization, work, investments, meditation, and prayer, by paying yourself first. You should also cultivate along the journey a deep appreciation and grace. The ultimate achievement of health and wealthness is going to be a grand encounter.

Remember:

Where focus goes energy flows.

Keep your focus on the future you and your energy will follow the path necessary to get there.

Do not compromise!

Keep the momentum rolling forward and above all, take massive action NOW!

...For more on how to achieve Health, Wealth & Wellness. I have included a plan in the Conclusion section of this book.

CHAPTER SIXTEEN

RETIRE AND MINE BITCOIN

This is not a book about retirement, but I thought I'd share my future plan on retirement income. Regardless of who you are, how old you are, or what area you work in, everyone at some point retires. Some people retire at death, and I certainly hope this is not you. Anyone who wants to retire from work before death at some point in their life must develop a strategic plan. People who don t have a strategic plan will find themselves unprepared for retirement and likely unable to afford the dream retirement they always imagined. Worse yet, they might be so financially unprepared that they must continue working against their will indefinitely, even till death.

The main reason a person cannot retire is finances and lack of necessary income to cover living expenses. Health and healthcare costs are the monsters in the closet. The explosion of cost in the golden years is unfathomable to the working youth.

Chapter Sixteen

When you're young and healthy you feel bulletproof and don't really grasp aging when health begins to fail. So most young people don't ever start planning their retirement. Regardless, a retirement plan is necessary. You must first realize that if you don't take this issue seriously, then your retirement income will be Social Security, but only if you worked and paid into it.

Okay, now slap yourself in the face again if you think Medicare will cover all your medical or health care needs. Feel that sting in your cheek? That's medical costs when you retire.

If your only source of income is Social Security you won't even be able to afford rent. The average Social Security benefit at the time of writing this book is $1,413.47 a month according to How Much You Will Get From Social Security by www.usnews.com. The maximum possible benefit retiring at age 70 is $2300 to $3700 depending on your yearly income. The more money you make in your working years the more Social Security benefit you earn in retirement. When a person retires at age 66 they get as low as $1826 a month to as high as $2861. So let's figure $1,413.47 is about right on for most working-class people who have actually labored most their life up until age 62. (The earliest a person can retire and collect Social Security is age 62 to receive a 75% benefit.) It's a tough choice to retire at a younger and likely healthier you at age 62 and accept a lesser benefit or hold out until age 70 and collect the maximum benefit. I personally hope I live to be 70 and very much look forward to retiring young not dead.

Now, considering the pathetic amount we will be getting from Social Security, it's obvious that after paying our rent or mortgage, utility bills, vehicle bills, food, water, gas, insurance policies, clothing, shoes, and other basic living essentials…Well, there's not a lot to go around. Now add in the luxuries in life, like cell phones, computers, tablets, TVs, Internet, cable, extra gas for travel, RVing, vacations, gifting, eating out, going to movies, etc. The list is endless for fun, enjoyable, and rewarding activities. This is the sugar on top that maximizes our quality of life, but it could be out of reach in retirement, when we have the most free time.

Now realize that all that I mentioned did not include healthcare. Why? Because most people don't consider healthcare and medical expenses when they are aging. It makes sense, I mean, why plan on something that doesn't exist yet and may not? Well, as a hospital therapist who has worked with thousands of patients over the years I can tell you first hand that disease and disability does not discriminate. I constantly work with people who cannot afford any "excessities" (My term for anything other the basic living expenses). They often live with their kids or in subsidized housing and can't afford a car, clothing, or going out to dinner due to lack of income and increased health and medical costs.

Based on what I have seen with retirees, medical expenses are the primo reason for losing everything. According to CNBC article: *Medical Bills Are the Biggest Cause of US Bankruptcies: Study.* **Healthcare is the No.1 cause of bankruptcies.**

By losing everything I mean all assets. I've met thousands of people who retire early and are now dead broke. They end up losing everything because, when they retire, their health fails and they need medical attention. They have no health insurance, so the medical bills wipe out any savings. Then they are forced to sell assets to pay off medical expenses until there are finely zero assets of value left. By all assets I am also referring to anything else of value, including 401(k), IRA, stocks, bonds, life insurance policies, rental properties, land, checking accounts, savings accounts, vehicles, and, yes, even your home. At the point of zero assets or wealth a retiree qualifies for Medicaid (joint Federal and state free or low-cost healthcare coverage). At this point a retiree has no chance of getting out of grinding poverty other than going back to work full time, getting a massive inheritance, or winning the lottery.

Chapter Sixteen

Being bankrupt and impoverished in retirement is preventable through early preparation. There are many things you can do about it. You can prepare for an early retirement by creating a perpetual monthly cash flow or income without working a typical job. An example for me is my rentals...I call each one a *money machine*. Rent income comes to me whether I work or not. A personal business can be a great money machine when you sell it on an owner sponsored loan or contract. The sale of a business can generate income with interest on into retirement and you don't have to work anymore. Royalties from an invention, patent, photography, artwork, or book can generate perpetual income and can be great money machines.

I have 19 years of experience working in acute care hospital rehabilitation. I have been working first hand with the aging and mostly retired generations. I have connected the dots and gained knowledge about retirement from an external perspective, interviewing thousands of patient retirees. This information is shared knowledge, knowledge passed on from my patients to me and now to you. I would like to share with you some trends that I have seen and lessons I have been taught by patients who have lived through it all already.

There are the haves and the have-nots when it comes to retirement and quality of life. The haves have invested in themselves, their health, and their wealthness. The have-nots have invested in everything but their health and/or wealth.

Both the haves and the have-nots worked and created cash flow up until retirement. The difference in the two after retirement is what matters. The haves and the have-nots both receive retirement income through Social Security benefits. But Social Security Income(SSI) is barely enough to scrape by. The haves invested in additional retirement income, which is paid monthly coming from 401(k) and IRA disbursements, rental property, stock dividends, owning their own assets, and having money in the bank. The have-nots only have their SSI

Chapter Sixteen

to live on and no means to increase their monthly cash flow other then returning to the workforce. If the have-nots are lucky, they paid off their home mortgage before retirement, otherwise they are renters for life or living with their kids.

From my external perspective, looking at thousands of patients' lives, choices, and retirement scenarios, I can state matter of factly that those with the most cash flow in retirement seem the happiest. They are content and keep moving toward their future goals. The have-nots stop moving forward at retirement. They seem to hit the brakes at retirement and live life at the mercy of their SSI income. The have-nots eventually lose any and all assets due to rising healthcare costs and economic inflation.

The good news is a person is never too old to start investing in themselves by eating well and exercising. In retirement, it is vital to keep one's health and wellness top priority in order to remain functional and prevent unnecessary healthcare costs.

For those of us who are working, we need to pay ourselves first and invest money for our future retirement. Unless someday you want to be a have-not then you need to take the massive action of the have-nows.

The future is the now! Invest the maximum you are able into a 401(k), IRA, HSA, penny stock, real estate, business, Internet marketing, e-commerce, websites, authoring books, inventions, cryptocurrencies, and, of course, Bitcoin.

Now we have another opportunity to create positive cash flow through Bitcoin mining. And why not Bitcoin mining in retirement? It's a voila! moment when one discovers another cash flow vehicle to add to their retirement arsenal.

In retirement we want to quit working and when we quit working, we stop earning money. Well Bitcoin mining is like working to earn money, except we don't have to do the work; the Bitcoin mining machines do all that.

After the initial investment of purchasing the miners,

Chapter Sixteen

the rack, PDUs, accessories, and electrical work, you have a Bitcoin mining operation. The Bitcoin mining operation does all the hashing twenty-four hours a day, seven days a week, with little maintenance required. At the cost of power your Bitcoin mining operation will continue to mine Bitcoins and deposit them into your wallet. Traditionally, Bitcoin mining is a positive cash flow operation with times of lower or higher returns, depending on the price of Bitcoin.

I am a Bitcoin miner now and plan to keep mining until the day I die. I am betting on, the Bitcoin future. I envision a Bitcoin world. I mine and invest in Bitcoin now, as I see the unlimited potential for growth over time. Bitcoin mining is a positive cash flow income stream for me now and will be a working cash flow vehicle into my retirement, along with my 401(k), IRA, HSA, and other savings and assets.

Why not? We only have one life to live and then we are dead. Why not embrace all the opportunities that intrigue us? When it comes to the haves and the have-nots, Bitcoin mining has traditionally been for the have-nots.

The have-nots have been mining Bitcoin since 2009, and now that Bitcoin has birthed its beautiful face to the world, the haves now want in. Big Banks, companies, governments, and the wealthy see the potential now and are investing. If Bitcoin becomes the world's digital gold standard, creating the world's first trillionaire and possibly future quadrillionaire, would you rather have Bitcoin or have not?

The risk is yours. Take this motto from the world's richest person, Jeff Bezos, owner of Amazon: "Minimize regret."

Regret minimization is Jeff's recommendation for achieving life success. He chooses to minimize any regret he has the opportunity to create. You create your own regret by not taking massive action toward your dreams and goals. When it comes to Bitcoin mining choose to minimize regret as I have.

So be merry! Be happy! Retire and become a Bitcoin miner.

CHAPTER SEVENTEEN

A VISIONARY BITCOIN MINERS PERSPECTIVE

The company Bitmain won't make founders Jihan Wu and Micree Zhan...the world's first quadrillionaires, but their holdings in Bitcoin and other cryptocurrency assets will. As Bitmain continues to pioneer Bitcoin mining, AI and VR technology, the sails remain open to catch the winds of exponential growth that Bitcoin will provide straight to the open seas of financial abundance.

The only way I can see Bitmain dethroned from top supplier of Bitcoin mining equipment is if a powerhouse tech company like Sony, Samsung, or Panasonic goes full throttle into cryptocurrency. I can see the future may hold a Samsung "Lightning" miner, running ultra-cool and power efficient at 250 TH. Wouldn't that be cool!

Another area of untapped mining power is through cell

phones and applications. There could be near 5 billion active cell phone users by the year 2019. Imagine the power of five billion cell phones combined, each running a Bitcoin and cryptocurrency mining or blockchain app. In fact, if one day all governments and nations of the earth go full digital currency, with blockchain the accountant for it all, it may become a requirement for all cell phones to run a background application supporting the blockchain and other financial infrastructure. This is a little farfetched, but someday when Bitcoin and cryptocurrencies are used in full force around the globe, five billion cell phones seems like a powerful yet untapped market to support a global financial system.

Remember my belief is that all governments, nations, continents, states, sectors, sects, clubs, and so on will each have their own custom cryptocurrency and blockchain. All these cryptocurrencies will trade among one another, using one source as a store of value: Bitcoin. Bitcoin will be the underlying infrastructure to maintain a solid, secure, incorruptible, unable to counterfeit, and universal measure of trading value and wealth.

The Internet is the now, the future, and Bitcoin the fuel to run it.

One coin to rule them all
One coin to find them
One coin to bring them all
And in the darkness bind them.

This is a parody I created, based off of the movie and book *Lord of the Rings*. I'm sure you all know the movie and the scene I'm spoofing. But if you don't, in the movie the verse refers to the one "ring of power" that holds domination over all other rings. In the story the leader of each race or nation of people

Chapter Seventeen

has a ring and each nation's ring is controlled or bound by the one true ring of power. Whoever holds the ring of power rules the middle earth.

We have great dependency on our current financial system. It is the process to earn, store, and trade wealth amongst one another. Presently the US dollar is the fiat currency of power in the world with all other nations currency bound by it. Bitcoin is the ring of power and all cryptocurrencies are the subservient coins representing each unique entity within the worldwide financial network. Whoever owns Bitcoin controls the world financial system. And what great power that will be!

There seem to be endless naysayers about Bitcoin, even among some of the wealthiest men on earth, like Warren Buffett. These seasoned and well-respected persons are stuck in their comfortable zone. They are pessimistic, ridicule, and down play Bitcoin and cryptocurrencies because they feel they have nothing to lose (or everything to lose). Warren Buffet was wrong about backing new technologies in the past. He dismissed the options to invest in Google and Amazon. Decisions Buffet regrets to this day (CNBC.com) We the youth have everything to gain. Bitcoin, cryptocurrencies, and blockchain will make more young millionaires than any other investment vehicle in the history of the world. Bitcoin will account for the biggest transfer of wealth the new millennia will ever witness.

Gamers, computer geeks, tech nerds, dreamers, visionaries, GenX, and millennials will likely make up the largest percentage of new millionaires. This is because they are open to new and better products, processes, and technologies to make our lives better. They are investing in Bitcoin, Bitcoin mining, cryptocurrencies, ICOs, business startups, application development, and building the technological infrastructure of our future system of financial accountability.

Chapter Seventeen

The Death of the Cell Phone

Is right around the corner...or at least to me seems like it should be.

When I was younger, in the late 1980s and early 1990s, we had phone booths on every street corner and landline corded phones in our homes. I remember when the cordless headset or cordless home phone came out and it was considered such a wonderful technological breakthrough. You still could not take the headset very far from the base unit or the connection would cut.

I remember when cell phones first became easily available for the public. I had one of the first cell phones among my friends. They were still sporting pagers. My first smartphone was the Motorola Timeport. I could send email but it was a painful laborious process. Searching the Internet was also tedious and inefficient. Now look all around us: smart phones are everywhere. The cell phone was the death of corded, cordless, and dial-up landline phone. Phone booths are in museums. You can't even find an old dial up or corded phone at garage sales anymore. Landlines are also about to be totally phased out. Just as dial-up and the landline have an expiration point, so does cellular. I believe the expiration of cellular is sooner than we think. When the death of cellular occurs, there may be a new turn of power from telecommunication giants like Sprint and Verizon to GPS and Wi-Fi controllers. With Wi-Fi and GPS encompassing the globe, I can see the future phone will be a Wi-Fi and GPS unit with long distance blue tooth capability. Traditional phone companies will be replaced by ISPs and application platforms for Wi-Fi, GPS, and Bluetooth communication.

Chapter Seventeen

The Death of Satellite and Cable TV is coming.

In fact, I can see all "hard line" tech expiring with the tech development and Wi-Fi infrastructure building up. All TV will be streamed via wireless Internet in the future.

Get ready to sell or upgrade all your 4K gadgets, because 8K is already out and knocking on the door.

Soon will be the death of pixel resolution and birth of Scalable Vector Graphics (SVG) in film, video, photography, and movies. Microsoft Word has just announced the ability to use Scalable Vector Images in its software. As this technology unfolds, so does VR. As VR unfolds, there may be a move from flat hard screen TVs to holographic or projected TVs that will support 360-degree VR media.

The Oculus Rift Go just released and out for Christmas of 2018 is a game changer. The Oculus Go can be used to play VR games, watch movies anywhere, communicate with friends and family, and a multitude of amazing other experiences.

When the cell phone dies and Wi-Fi is used for most intercommunications then tech devices like the Oculus Rift Go can be used to make VR phone calls or join chat rooms. The Oculus Go only costs $250 compared to the price of a cell phone like the iPhone X at just over a grand!

Video gaming always seems to be on the forefront of graphics technology, as gamers constantly desire and seek an improved game play experience. If you want to know the future of computer technology and computer sciences, then monitor what is happing in video gaming. VR gaming has been here, is developing, and will take over the visual experience as we know it. The future holds VR TV, VR movies, VR driving, VR flying, and VR communications. Someday we will be looking at a 360-degree holographic VR image of the person or group of persons we are talking to. And it could be coming from a watch, portable device, headset, or implanted microchip. From smart phone to smart chip!

Artificial Intelligence (AI) is taking over control or interfaces between people and their tech. AI is here and growing at an exponential rate right before our eyes. AI is in all social media and search engine interfaces, Amazon, Google, Bing, Yahoo, Facebook, Instagram, YouTube, Tumbler, LinkedIn, are all an AI interface between you and tech. Governments, nations, corporations, financial systems, real estate, you name it, they're all using artificial intelligence. The subject of AI is vast and complex. If you are interested in more information on just how deep the rabbit hole of AI goes then I recommend reading the book, *The Master Algorithm* by Pedro Domingos.

The Death of News Media as we know it is unfolding.

CNN, FOX, CBS, NBC, MSNBC, ABC are all slowly but surely losing hold on average citizens. People want the truth. We want real stories about real people and want to make our own decisions about topics based on the facts.

The replacement to the big mass media controllers are the Internet and we the people. Anyone can, in a matter of minutes, setup and host a live stream event on or off site. Social media and live streaming is the future of news.

I can see at some point in the future there will be millions of people around the globe positioned in every city and neighborhood, all with Internet and portable live-streaming capability. When an event happens, there will be many people already recording or live streaming the news event before the big media outlets can even think of sending their reporters on site. In fact, this is already happening and on the verge of taking over.

This is where AI comes in. Someday someone will create an algorithm that monitors all global social media outlets, all websites, basically the entire Internet of things, for current live

Chapter Seventeen

news feeds. There could be many different algorithms doing this, each trying to be the biggest news provider. But when it comes down to it, the live stream or recording is owned by the person who creates it, and it will have to be paid for. We may all have opportunities to get paid as news media reporters someday.

I want to watch The Good News or Inspiring News Channel. I mean, there are a lot of good things happening on this earth and it would be nice to know or hear about this news, in addition to all the bad, negative, or evil doings that are going on in our world.

Come On! Let's have it!

Please, someone create a positive news media outlet:
The Good News Channel.

I'll subscribe...

Chapter Seventeen

CONCLUSION

I can't wait to read the headlines: "World's First Trillionaire!" Someday we may see the world's first trillionaire or quadrillionaire born from Bitcoin investments and blockchain development.

Watch as GenX, Gen Y, and GenZ harness, accept, and passionately build the world's infrastructure for blockchain communications and financial operations.

Watch as the Winklevoss twins become so wealthy, they buy and gain control of Facebook from Zuckerberg with their pocket change.

Remember to keep your finger on the pulse. Be poised to invest in the next tech company that will push Bitcoin and cryptocurrencies to the next level.

Watch for Bitcoin apps, businesses, blockchain companies, and blockchain platforms.

Open your eyes and the eyes of your friends and family to Bitcoin and its obvious foothold in the global financial system. Bitcoin is everyone's chance at owning some of the wealth pie. Take a slice or a bite before its too late.

And, by golly, make it a point to visit central Washington,
specifically Douglas County,
The Bitcoin Capital of the World.
You won't regret it.

Bitcoin / bit.coin (bit-,koin): *The coin of power*. The universal accepted store of value. The tie that binds all cryptocurrencies, fiats, and money. (i.e. the replacement of gold as a store of value).

Bitcoin is the next big thing since the invention of the Internet. It provides low cost, anonymous, permissionless, and low fraud transactions. Bitcoin is a decentralized form of currency without a central bank. Bitcoin is open source, of limited supply and at no risk of inflation. Bitcoin is Freedom.

One coin to rule them all
One coin to find them
One coin to bring them all
...and in the darkness bind them.

The Bitcoin Capital of the World...Ha!... In my house!

John Van Leyden

BONUS MATERIAL

Conclusion

The JVL Adventure List

"A PERSONAL TOUR OF THE BITCOIN CAPITAL OF THE WORLD"

• •

Leavenworth: A grand place to take the family for a rewarding and memorable experience. If you can try to time your visit to Leavenworth during one of the major festivals like the Bavarian Icefest, Maifest, Bavarian bike and brew, Autumn Leaf Festival (my favorite), Oktoberfest (all beer lovers favorite), and the Christmas Lighting Festival (a whole family favorite).

Leavenworth has a plethora of annual outdoor activities ranging from a multitude of hiking trails, rock climbing, river rafting and tubing, road and mountain biking, nature walks, camping, fishing, hunting, etc. I guarantee you'll have an amazing outdoor experience in some of the most beautiful county you've ever seen. All only a few minutes from town.

There are many bed and breakfasts, hotels, and Air BNBs, or camping accommodations. If camping I recommend being early (early bird gets the worm) and staying in one of the campgrounds up Icicle creek…my favorite, "Bridge Creek."

Conclusion

Bridge creek is far enough up the icicle to feel deep in the wilderness and close to the eight mile trailhead, which is one of my favorite day hikes that kids over 6 can enjoy without much difficulty. Prepare for and/or anticipate the moment you crest out of the trail and into view of the lake...wow, breathtaking.

Downtown Leavenworth has a cornucopia of things to do as far as shopping, eating, drinking, dancing, live music, ice cream shops, and more shopping. You will see many people in Bavarian dress including dirndls, lederhosen, and other nutcracker like apparel. I recommend lunch, coffee, and cookies at the Gingerbread shop and dinner at the Munchen Haus...ohhh this is making me hungry! If you still have room have a fresh scooped ice cream cone from one of the many ice cream, pastry, and candy shops. There are many pubs, wine venues, and breweries to enjoy.

If you like to ski there is a small ski are in Leavenworth called Leavenworth Ski Hill and if you want more a more epic skiing experience then Steven's Pass, owned by Vail Resorts lies just 30-40 minutes away. Steven's pass is one of the best ski resorts I have experienced. Steven's Pass resort also has an epic mountain biking park during the non-snow months. Check out one of my favorite Leavenworth marketing videos on YouTube: www.youtube.com/watch?v=unQz4kFJ2Tg (*Woody Goomsba!*)

Pybus Market: A fun place to stop in Wenatchee for shopping, lunch or dinner, live music, coffee, wine, beer, and other seasonal events. I recommend bringing some extra money to spend at one of the many vendors, shops, or table setups. My wife's favorite place to eat at Pybus is the South, where you can enjoy authentic Latin food and beverages from Central and South American. My favorite is "Almond Blossom" nut store. Another fun activity is to rent bikes from Arlberg and ride around the Apple Capital Loop Trail (a 10 mile paved route

Conclusion

from Wenatchee to East Wenatchee and back).

Wenatchee (The Apple Capital of the World): Right across the Columbia river from The Bitcoin Capital of the World lies Wenatchee. Other then the Pybus market, which is located in downtown Wenatchee there are many checklist items here. Experience the historic downtown culture where you can enjoy a variety of shopping, dining, and live music. I recommend taking a dive into Collins Fashions, Cafe Mela, and don't miss the Owl Soda Fountain and Gifts shop.

There are many hiking and biking trails just on the outskirts of Wenatchee that are good exercise, fun, and rewarding. My favorites are Saddlerock, Sage Hills, the Mission Ridge trail, and Devil's Gulch. The ultimate is to mountain bike down from the top of Devil's Gulch to the bottom, which comes out Mission creek in Cashmere, WA. If you like to ski then Mission Ridge ski resort is just about 20 minutes away.

A not very publicized and personal favorite is to drive to the Stemilt Loop road and hike, mountain bike, or ATV the many green dot roads. Also on the Stemilt Loop road there are 3 lakes that are fun to take the family for a quick outing to enjoy small lakeside relaxation, fishing, or swimming. They are Black Lake, Lily Lake, and Clear Lake...enjoy!

Lake Chelan: A great summer destination for family fun. Enjoy swimming at the state parks, boating, water skiing, paragliding, para-sailing, jet skiing, you name it water activity. There are many hotels and campgrounds to stay in. I recommend booking a trip on the Lady of the Lake to Stehekin (a small village secluded on the other side of the 50 mile long lake).

At Stehekin you can enjoy camping, cabin rentals, are just a day visit. When in Stehekin take the local tour and then rent bikes or hike to the Stehekin Pastry Company that lies just a ways. At the Stehekin Pastry Company enjoy great fresh

Conclusion

from scratch foods, deserts, and ice cream. Don't forget your mosquito spray! Just in case.

Rocky Reach Dam: This is a great family place to stop for a picnic and go on a guided tour of the hydroelectric dam. You get to see some of the history of the area and the inner workings of a dam and how the work.

The Quincy Lakes: There are many little to medium sized lakes in this area. A local favorite is to take a hike into Ancient or Dusty lake. Enjoy beautiful views, fishing, bird watching, and pack for a picnic.

The Gorge Amphitheatre: A fun place to enjoy live music. If you can coordinate your trip to stop and enjoy a concert here you won't regret it. The venue offers breathtaking views as the backdrop for the stage and live events. There are primitive campgrounds spots available and RV spots. I recommend trying to book a spot in Crescent Bar, which is just a hop skip and a jump from the Gorge.

Highlander Golf Course: In East Wenatchee lies a this golfing experience. Enjoy breathtaking scenery while you golf then have a great meal or beverage at the clubhouse.

Wine Tours: From Walla Walla to Oroville and on into Penticton then into Kelowna Canada is draped in a blanket of Wineries, wine tours, and wine tasting. My favorite wine tours are in and around Lake Chelan and then if really adventurous take a wine tasting tour from Penticton to Kelowna Canada. Don't forget to bring a designated driver for this trip.

Conclusion

Health, Wealth, & Wellness

"HEALTH & WEALTHNESS PLAN"

Let's talk about the components of health for a bit here. The components are...

—**physical** (health of our bodies),

—**mental** (health of thoughts, emotions, and behavior), and

—**spiritual** (sense of being, our connectedness, beliefs, religion, sense of right and wrong, morality, and higher purpose).

The physical component of health is mostly within our control and greatly influences the mental and spiritual components. We control the types, quantity, and timing of foods we eat. We control the types, quantity, and timing of our exercise activity. When it comes to the physical component of health, the owner of your body (you!) has complete control over the fuel and the workload, AKA food and exercise.

Now for the topic of health and wealthness, I'll only touch on the most important aspects of my famous K.I.S.S. motto

Conclusion

(Keep It Simple, Silly) when it comes to eating and exercise. There are thousands of books on dieting, nutrition, exercise, weight training, etc. I recommend you go on to read as much as you can on the subjects you have questions about. A book that I have read and provided great information is Exercise Rx by Gary Yanker. For the components of health, I am giving you my opinion and advice based on 22 years of experience in the areas of bodybuilding, weight training, power lifting, dieting, competition, and work as a CFT (Certified Fitness Instructor) and licensed Occupational Therapist. I am breaking it all down to the nitty gritty, what I know from experience matters most and will actually work.

"You are what you eat," I tell my patients. This is absolutely true and key to every single person's success in earning a lean and healthy physique.

If you eat fat, then you are fat.
If you eat protein, then you are muscle.
If you eat carbohydrates, then you are energized.

What you choose to eat should complement your needs. If you are overweight, then the last thing you need is fat or energy. You have enough stored in your skin's fat layer and should use that fuel before consuming more. If you are too thin and weak, then you need more muscles and energy but want lean body mass not fat body mass so eat more protein foods and starchy carbs. If you are in great shape already or have achieved a healthy lean physique, then you need a balance of fat, protein, and carbohydrates (fat, muscles, energy) that promote maintenance of a lean healthy physique.

Let's look closer at the three physique types we just talked about and set the goals for each.

Conclusion

K.I.S.S. (Keep It Simple, Silly)

1. Fat/Overweight (Endomorph): Thick Framed ...*NFL Lineman*. To improve health this body type needs to lose body fat. Your goal should be to burn off body fat until lean. This body type needs to eat lean protein and vegetables and eliminate sugars, fats, and minimize carbohydrates to allow thermogenesis or fat burning to occur.

Goal: Fat burning and muscle sparing until a lighter, leaner, and stronger physique is attained.

*Calorie breakdown for this body type to promote fat burning/thermogenesis: 60% protein, 35% fibrous vegetables and restricted low glycemic complex carbohydrates. (no sugars), 5% fats.

2. Skinny/or skinny fat (Ectomorph): The Hardgainer... *NBA basket ball player*. This body type needs to try to gain muscle mass and prevent adding body fat. This type needs to eat an overabundance of lean protein, vegetables, and carbohydrate sources to provide energy to prevent muscle breakdown and protein to promote muscle synthesis or growth.

Goal: Gain lean body mass until a heavier, but lean and strong physique is attained.
*Calorie breakdown for this body type: 50% protein, 45% carbohydrates, and 5% fats.

3. Lean Physique (Mesomorph): The Athletic Average... *NFL receiver or professional soccer player*. This body type needs to eat a balance of lean protein sources, vegetables, and complex carbohydrates.

Conclusion

Goal: Maintenance of a lean strong physique

*Calorie breakdown: 60% protein, 35% mix of low glycemic complex starchy and fibrous carbohydrates, and 5% fat.

For all 3 body types I recommend a focus on:

—**Prevent gaining body fat at all costs.**

—**Prevent muscle loss at all costs.**

—**Promote fat burning consistently.**

—**Promote muscle synthesis and maintain or raise muscle strength.**

For all three physique types, I recommend some of the following basic rules:

Rule #1: Stay far from or eliminate deserts, candy, chocolate, donuts, muffins, cakes, sugary syrups, and sugar. These types of foods have slim to zero nutritional value for your body and will only get you fatter fast.

Rule #2: Eat a boat load of vegetables. Vegetables are low calorie in general and full of nutritional value. You can't really eat too much fibrous vegetables. So consume, consume, consume.

Rule #3: Always eat lean foods. Stay away from anything that is not lean. Basically, try to eliminate fats from your diet and supplement or cook with healthy oils like olive or canola. You can also supplement with fish oil and omegas.

Conclusion

Rule #4: Eat lean protein sources as the main staple of every meal of the day. An easy way to consume adequate amounts of protein a day is to use whey protein powder. If you are a strict Vegetarian or Vegan your options for quality protein are slim and lower on the Biological Value (BV) scale but remain nonetheless and some good options are beans, tofu, yogurt, grains, and soy.

Rule #5: Limit intake of alcohol drinks. Drinking alcohol in excess will make you fat, make you feel like crap the next day, and has slim to zero nutritional value for your body. If you are going to consume alcoholic drinks, choose the low calorie options like light or low calorie beers, wines, or malt liquors. Stay away from mixed alcohol and sugary drinks. These will only make you fatter.

Rule #6: *Fruits are tricky.* Yes, they are nutritious and healthy, but how much fruit you should consume, if any, depends on your goals. If you are trying to lose body fat, then you should limit or eliminate fruits from your diet until you achieve your desired body type and supplement fiber in other means like Metamucil wafers. Fruits are sugar. Sugars prevent thermogenesis, AKA fat burning. If you are already lean and fit then consume fruits for nutritional value.

Rule #7: Last meal of the day. This is a crucial time of the day to eat or not to eat. It depends on your goals. If your goal is to lose body fat, then your last food intake should be two to three hours before bedtime. If your goal is maintenance of your current physique, then your last food intake should be one to two hours before bedtime. If your goal is to gain weight or muscle, then your last food intake should be 30 to 60 minutes before bed.

Conclusion

Rule #8: Try to break down your calories for the day into five to seven smaller meals rather than the traditional two to three meals a day. Here's my routine, and take in mind I wake up between 3 or 4 a.m. For example: a 40-gram whey protein shake first thing in the morning, followed by another one two hours later, followed by a 12 egg (2 yolk and 12 whites) omelet with veggies, then another 40-gram whey protein shake 2 hours later, and then lunch. Lunch is usually the same thing most days: meat and veggies. Then, after work or in the afternoon, I get in a good workout, outdoor activity, or exercise. After my workout I always have a post workout protein shake. Then about one hour after my late afternoon workout I have dinner, which is a modest portion of meat, vegetables, and complex carbohydrates. This is how I manage to break down my calories for the day into seven smaller portions. I mix my whey protein shakes with water only to avoid the excess calories and sugars in milks. I buy bags of frozen vegetables and prepare my lunches ahead of times for the week. I add meats and vegetables to meal storage dishes and put them in the freezer. For my egg breakfast, I work at a hospital, so I buy my scrambled eggs there and on days off I cook them myself at home. Eggs are easy and quick to prepare. For dinner I try to cook something yummy, or if I'm in a pinch for time (which is most of the time), then I just nuke some lean frozen precooked meats and vegetables.

Rule #9: Know your Basal Metabolic Rate (BMR) and plan your daily calories to meet your physique goals. Your daily calorie requirement should promote your goal of fat loss, maintenance, or weight gain. First, to figure out your BMR, I recommend using the Harris Benedict Equation. You can calculate using the formula yourself or use a BMR calculator like the one at the Ideal Protein website (idealprotein.com) Once you know your BMR, you can figure out your daily

Conclusion

caloric intake needs. The BMR calculator at idealprotein.com will also give you an estimate of your daily calorie needs. Sounds redundant, but please read on.

BMR: Your caloric need in a restful state of being, i.e. if I do nothing other than breath, sleep, eat, and self-care today, then this is how many calories I need at a minimum to avoid tissue breakdown within my body. Daily Caloric Requirement: your BMR, plus any extra calorie needs for workouts, exercise, competitions, work, and any other activities that increase the demand for fuel(calories), thus increasing your overall eating to avoid tissue breakdown and provide the power or energy for the physical activity at hand. To lose body fat we need to consume less calories then we are burning in order to promote the burning of body fat rather than food calories. If you're overweight, you'll want a calorie deficit. For those who want to maintain a lean healthy physique, then a caloric intake around the daily caloric intake recommendation will be the goal. For those who need to gain weight or add muscle, then you need to consume more than the daily recommended caloric intake. If you're underweight, you will want an excess of calories.

Rule #10: Don't cheat! Be disciplined toward your goals, and when you achieve them, celebrate but maintain. Cheating leads to losing, failure, and eventually giving up entirely. ***Cheaters NEVER prosper*** for the long term.

Exercise or physical activity is a powerful tool we can use at our discretion. We control our engagement in activity or not. We have total control of our bodies and what activity we choose to participate in. Research has proven over and over again that exercise, fitness, cardiovascular activity, and weight training improve one's health. The benefits of exercise are improved weight control and reduced risk of heart disease. It helps your body manage blood sugars and insulin levels, improves mental

Conclusion

health and mood, strengthens your bones and muscles, reduces risk of some cancers, reduces risk of falling, improves sexual function, improves quality of sleep, promotes brain activity, and improves your chances of living longer.

Exercise is engaging in an activity that increases your heart rate enough to matter. Exercise is recruiting muscles to work to move your body. Exercise increases the speed of workload of muscles and body movements.

Here's a myth I run into all the time: Walking is exercise. No! Walking is a basic low-threshold activity that barely raises the heart rate and has the only benefit of being slightly better than a resting state at best. So yes, walking is better than nothing, but it is not exercise (unless walking is difficult for the person due to aging, obesity, or other debility). In those instances, walking can be considered exercise, but will need to be of considerable duration to have a therapeutic benefit.

For exercise, I recommend any activity that you enjoy, increases your heart rate, and forces your body to work. My favorite, due to ease of use, convenience at home, and availability at all gyms, is the elliptical trainer. The elliptical trainer is easy on the joints and promotes an elevated heart rate, and you can adjust the resistance or workload to your needs. There are probably a million forms of exercise. Use your imagination and check your heart rate mid-activity to see if it's working. I recommend the book "The Men's Fitness Exercise Bible: 101 Best Workouts To Build Muscle, Burn Fat, and Sculpt Your Best Body Ever!"

Weight training is important in maintaining or adding lean muscle tissue and strengthening. I can't think of any negative aspect of being strong. People admire, idolize, and are motivated by strong men and women. The word strong in itself is powerful enough to warrant weight training to improve one's strength. I mean who wouldn't want to be described as strong?

Weight training also promotes anabolism or growth of new

Conclusion

muscle tissue. This kind of weight training must be at a higher workload and intensity to cause muscle tissue to breakdown, then the body will respond by making muscles bigger.

Another myth: If I lift weights, I'll get too big. Good grief, give me a break! This one's total BS. Ask any person NOT taking steroids how easy it is to gain muscle, cause it isn't easy. It is extremely difficult and time consuming. Consider yourself disciplined and blessed if you notice a gain in lean body mass. Actually pat yourself on the back (if you can still reach it), because it is proof that you have been killing it in the gym for quite some time. Weight training has other therapeutic effects like increased overall muscle tone, increased metabolism, fat burning, decreased mental stress, and improved mood.

Exercise and weight training are obviously great tools and necessary to achieve an overall healthy state of being. I recommend general exercise daily for 30 minutes or more. Exercise can take many different forms, from running on a treadmill to hiking up a mountain, as long as you're raising your heart rate, increasing overall workload, and exerting force or effort. For weights, I recommend training each muscle once a week. How many days a week depends on your goals. If your goal is general health, then you could get one long session in and get every muscle in one day, called circuit training. I recommend against this and prefer two or more weight training sessions split by muscle groups. For a two-day-a-week routine, you can split your workouts into upper (waist up) and lower body (waist down) on separate days. In general, a two-day split is the best for most people. As a bodybuilder I aim to complete three to five weight training sessions a week and split my muscle groups up into Arms, Back, Chest, Shoulders, and Leg Day. This allows more time to focus on individual muscle groups, and with that greater gains or improvements in strength and lean body mass. Okay, now go lift something and move it. Voila! You're on the road to health.

Conclusion

In all that you do on the path to achieving ultimate health and wealthness, it is important to cater to the wellness of your entire being. Your wellness involves your thoughts, emotions, and sense of well-being or being centered. The journey of life can be a trial full of stressful, painful, and sad encounters. There will also be many happy, elating, rewarding, and peaceful moments. The ability to experience the good and tolerate the bad depends on your skills of relaxation, re-centering, and re-thinking. There are many tools we can use to achieve this sense of balance.

From your personal trainer and life coach...

"May God bless you with health, wealth, and wellness. May he give you the strength to achieve your dreams in this precious life."

John Van Leyden

BIBLE VERSES RELATED TO HEALTH, WEALTH, MINING/GOLD, AND WELLNESS

Gold
Exodus 20:23
Psalm 119:127

Health
3 John 1:2
Proverbs 31:17

Wealth
Hebrews 13:5
Deuteronomy 8:18

Wellness
1 Corinthians 9:26-27
Matthew 22:37

Compaq server rack loaded with 12-Bitmain Antminer S9s...My spring 2018 upgrade.

1 Cisco Blade 48 channel network switch between...

2 Dell Servers Below

Ethereum mining rig with custom aluminum frame, 8 video cards, and all assessories.

There are many of these Bitcoin ATMs throughout the Seattle Corridor.

RESOURCES/REFERENCES AND RECOMMENDATIONS

Geissinger, Eric. (2016). Virtual Billions: The Genius, the Drug Lord, and the Ivy League Twins behind the Rise of Bitcoin. Amherst, NY: Prometheus Books.

Wiley, John & Sons Inc. (2016). Bitcoin For Dummies. Hoboken, New Jersey: John Wiley & Sons, Inc.

Laurence, Tiana. (2017). Blockchain For Dummies. Hoboken, New Jersey: John Wiley & Sons, Inc.

Robbins, Anthony. (2014). Money Master The Game 7 Simple Steps To Financial Freedom. New York, NY: Simon & Schuster Paperbacks.

Robbins, Anthony & Mallouck, Peter. (2017). UNSHAKEABLE Your Financial Freedom Playbook Creating Peace Of Mind In A World Of Volatility. New York, NY: Simon & Schuster, Inc.

Kiyosaki, Robert T & Lechter, Sharon L. (1998). Rich Dad Poor Dad. What the Rich Teach Their Kids about Money-That the Poor and Middle Class Do Not! New York, NY: Warner Books.

Kiyosaki, Robert T. (2011). UNFAIR advantage The Power Of Financial Education. What Schools Will NEVER Teach You About Money. Scottsdale, AZ: Plata Publishing, LLC.

Kiyosaki, Robert T. (2013). Why "A" Students Work For "C" Students and "B" Students Work For The Government. Scottsdale, AZ: Plata Publishing, LLC.

Sutton, Garrett, ESQ & Kiyosaki, Robert T. (2003). How to Buy & Sell a Business. How You Can Win in the Business Quadrant. New York, NY: Warner Books, Inc.

Ross, George H, McLean, Andrew James & Trump, Donald J. (2005). Trump Strategies For Real Estate. Billionaire Lessons for the Small Investor. Hoboken, New Jersey: John Wiley & Sons Inc.

Domingos, Pedro. (2015). The Master Algorithm. How The Quest For The Ultimate Learning Machine Will Remake Our World. New York, NY: Basic Books of Perseus Books, LLC.

Zelinski, Ernie J. (2016). How To Retire Happy, Wild, and Free. Retirement wisdom that you won't get from your financial advisor. Edmonton, AB, Canada: Visions International Publishing.

Bronchick, William, Esq. & Dahlstrom, Robert. (2006). Flipping Properties. Second Edition. Generate Instant Cash Profits in Real Estate. Chicago, IL: Kaplan Publishing.

Palin, Sarah. (2010). America By Heart. Reflections on Family, Faith, and Flag. New York, NY: HarperCollins Publishers.

Ciampa, Rob, Moore, Theresa & Carucci, John. (2015). YouTube Channels For Dummies. Hoboken, New Jersey: John Wiley & Sons Inc.

Ramsey, Dave. (2011). EntreLeadership. New York, NY: Howard Books a Division of Simon & Schuster, Inc.

Vaynerchuk, Gary. (2016). #ASKGARYVEE. One Entrepreneur's Take on Leadership, Social Media & Self-Awareness. New York, NY: HarperCollins Publishers.

Vaynerchuk, Gary. (2018). CRUSHING IT! How Great Entrepreneurs Build Their Business and Influence-And How You Can, Too. New York, NY: HarperCollins Publishers.

Daymond, John. (2018). Rise and Grind. Outperform, Outwork, and Outhustle Your Way To A More Successful And Rewarding Life. New York, NY: Crown Publishing Group, a division of Penguin Random House LLC.

Dipazza, Daniel. (2017). Rich20Something. Ditch Your Average Job. Start An Epic Business And Score The Life You Want. New York, NY: Penguin Random House LLC.

Yanker, Gary. (1999). Exercise Rx. The Lifetime Prescription for Reducing Medical Risks and Sports Injuries. New York, NY: Kodansha America, Inc.

Schwarzenegger, Arnold & Hall, Douglas Kent. (1979). Arnold's Bodyshaping for Women. A Complete Program for a Lifetime of Fitness and Beauty. New York, NY: Simon & Schuster Publishing.

Schwarzenegger, Arnold. (1999). The New Encyclopedia of Modern Bodybuilding. The Bible of Bodybuilding, Fully Updated and Revised. New York, NY: Simon & Schuster Inc.

Wurman, Richard Saul, Siegel, Alan & Morris, Kenneth M. (1989). The Wall Street Journal Guide to Understanding Money& Markets Stocks/Bonds/Mutual Funds/Futures/Money. New York, NY: AccessPress Ltd. a division of Simon & Schuster, Inc.

Eker, T. Harv. (2005). Secrets of the Millionaire Mind. Mastering the Inner Game of Wealth. New York, NY: HarperCollins Publishing, Inc.

McDaniels, Nevonne. (2018). Bitcoin prices take a dramatic dip. Wenatchee, WA: The Wenatchee World.

McDaniels, Nevonne. (2018). PUD boosts security as denied bitcoin miners turn belligerent. Wenatchee, WA: The Wenatchee World.

McDaniels, Nevonne. (2018). PUD considers new rate option for backyard bitcoin miners. Wenatchee, WA: The Wenatchee World.

McDaniels, Nevonne. (2018). Crypto-currency rates get November hearing. Wenatchee, WA: The Wenatchee World.

Mire, Bridget. (2018). PUD approves new cryptocurrency rates. Wenatchee, WA: The Wenatchee World.

McDaniels, Nevonne. (2018). Carlson steps down, staff let go. Wenatchee WA: The Wenatchee World.

McDaniels, Nevonne. (2018). Mining is part of recovery. Wenatchee, WA: The Wenatchee World.

Buhr, Tony. (2018). Giga Watt declares bankruptcy. Wenatchee, WA: The Wenatchee World.

Buhr, Tony. (2018). Bitcoin operation opens near airport. Wenatchee, WA: The Wenatchee World.

WEB REFERENCES AND RECOMMENDED SITES

https://bitmain.com
https://giga-watt.com
https://en.wikipedia.org/wiki/Bitmain
https://en.wikipedia.org/wiki/Cryptocurrency
https://aws.amazon.com/partners/blockchain
https://en.wikipedia.org/wiki/history_of_bitcoin
https://douglaspud.org/Documents/Feb%20Rates%202018
https://gemini.com
https://bitcoin.org
https://coinbase.com/charts
https://bittrex.com
https://grayscale.co/bitcoin-investment-trust/
https://ledger.com
https://sec.gov
https://coindesk.com/sec
https://coin-etf.com
https://coinme.com
https://bitcoin.com/bitcoin-atm/
https://money.cnn https://foxbusiness.com

INDEX

4

401(k) · 80

A

Accounting ledger · 76
AI · 116
Altcoins · 71
Amazon · 116
Antminer · 66
Arnold Schwarzenegger · XIII
Artificial Intelligence · 116
Asset · II
Assets · XVIII

B

Bank · 13
Bill Gates · 3
Bitcoin · III
Bitcoin blockchain · 75
Bitcoin development · 13
Bitcoin mining · 43
Bitmain · 111
Blockchain · 75
BTC · VI
Business · 9
Business · 99

C

College · 6
Commodity · 15
Craigslist · 81
Currencies · 12
Currency · 13

D

Digital currency · 13
Douglas County · VIII

E

ETF · 59
Evolution of money · 11
Exercise · 95

F

Fast money · 70
Fiat · 12
Fund · 59

G

Giga Watt · 53
Google · 57
Government · III
Grayscale · 69

H

Health · 94
Health & wealthness · 92
Health, wealth, and wellness · 92
Healthcare · 51
Highlander · 126
HSA · 94

I

IBM · I
IRA · 94

L

Lake Chelan · 125
Leavenworth · 123
Ledger · 37

M

Mark Zuckerberg · 3
Microsoft · I
Miner · 27
Money · 11

P

PC gaming · XVI
PDU · 31
Penny Stocks · 98
Property · 95
Pybus Market · 124

R

Real Estate · 95
Retire · 105

S

Satoshi Nakamoto · 13
Social Media · 100
Social Security · 106
Spondoolies · 27
Stock market · 98
Store of value · 84

T

The Bitcoin Capital of the World · 49
The Gorge Amphitheatre · 126
The Quincy Lakes · 126

U

Unlimited potential · II
USD/BTC · VI

W

Wallet · 41
Wealth · 92
Wenatchee · 53
Wine · 126
Winklevoss · 58

John Van Leyden is an American author living in the Bitcoin capital of the world. Where the Bitcoin flows from the power lines like honey from a hive. He rose from the ashes of hellfire, which to him is poverty, to being a successful career professional, investor, and Bitcoin miner.

John wants to share his knowledge and life experiences as well as the inside strategies and secrets to become a successful Bitcoin miner, get in shape, and achieving a life of maximal health and wealthness.

Join the JVL blog @ www.thebitcoincapital.com
Stay current on the status of Bitcoin!

Would you like to contribute to or sponsor the work that goes into building the website and the JVL blog? Any help to establish and maintain the website is much appreciated. Of note the JVL blog is a for-profit organization. Contributions, sponsorship, or donations are not tax deductible or refundable.

Donate/Sponsor in Bitcoin (BTC)…

Receiving BTC Address:
3DRwZhqz8rjmTLJpGQtFgrLaNvx33tpvYc

Contact Information: bitcoincapitaloftheworld@gmail.com

Finally, please consider leaving a review online.
It will help promote this book and support myself…*John Van Leyden* to write more books to come.

Thank you

JVL

www.ingramcontent.com/pod-product-compliance
Lightning Source LLC
Chambersburg PA
CBHW052032070526
44584CB00016B/2012